D0532629

Some Modern Faiths

(second edition)

*Maurice C. Burrell
& J. Stafford Wright*

Inter-Varsity Press

Inter-Varsity Press
38 De Montfort Street, Leicester LE1 7GP, England

First edition 1973
Reprinted 1974
Second edition 1983
Reprinted 1984

British Library Cataloguing in Publication Data
Burrell, Maurice C.
    Some modern faiths—2nd ed.
    1. Religions, Modern
    I. Title   II. Wright, J. Stafford
    289   BL98

ISBN 0-85110-433-9

Typeset in 10/11 pt Baskerville
Phototypeset by Nuprint Services Ltd., Harpenden, Herts.
Printed and bound in Great Britain by Collins, Glasgow

Inter-Varsity Press is the publishing division of the Universities and Colleges Christian Fellowship (formerly the Inter-Varsity Fellowship), a student movement linking Christian Unions in universities and colleges throughout the United Kingdom and the Republic of Ireland, and a member movement of the International Fellowship of Evangelical Students. For information about local and national activities write to UCCF, 38 De Montfort Street, Leicester LE1 7GP.

Contents

Preface

This book is a completely revised and updated edition of *Some Modern Faiths,* which was first published in 1973, and it also contains some additional material. Since 1973, a number of modern religious cults have been actively proselytizing in the western world. Maurice Burrell has examined seven of these in *The Challenge of the Cults,* which was first published in 1981. Despite the widespread concern caused by these more recent religious propagandists and the full coverage given to their activities by the media, it is still largely from the more established sects examined in *Some Modern Faiths* that the mainstream Christian churches face a more vigorous challenge. So this book takes another and an updated look at these established sects, most of which originated in North America in the nineteenth century.

We have tried to be unemotional and factual in our presentation of the basis of each of the sects we have examined, and have then attempted to show how each differs from mainstream Christianity. We have endeavoured to be scrupulously fair and have avoided snap answers to views with which we have disagreed. If, however, despite our efforts, we have misrepresented any of the sects we have examined, we should like to be informed in order that we may make any necessary corrections in subsequent editions.

At this point the position from which we write should be stated clearly. We have written from the point of view of those who believe that in the Bible we have God's true revelation of himself, and not simply one more record of man's search for God. That being so, we have treated the

Bible as the yardstick against which to measure both our own views and those of the sects we have examined. A sceptic might point to the divisions in the churches and say that the Bible can be made to support any view: we ourselves are well aware of the fact that the sects themselves quote the Bible in support of their beliefs and practices.

We readily confess the sinfulness of the divisions within mainstream Christianity, and while we rejoice at all moves towards Christian unity, we do not wish in any way to play down the differences that still exist between the churches. What we wish to make clear, however, is that such differences are largely peripheral. When it comes to the fundamental issues of the nature of God and what he has done in Christ to save fallen mankind, the Christian churches are in agreement.

Our position, then, is that which all the churches, Catholic, Orthodox and Protestant, including the denominational churches, have always regarded as the truth about the being of God and the divine action for our salvation as drawn from Scripture, although some modern scepticism about the final authority of the Bible has naturally affected concepts of God and Christ.

In contrast, the sects in this book which claim to be based on the Bible have come to birth in comparatively recent times and hold that the whole Christian church has got it wrong, and that it has in fact been in fundamental error in its understanding of the biblical revelation for the best part of nineteen centuries. The scales must be weighted against such extreme views, though this in itself does not rule out the possibility (however remote) that one or other of these alternatives to orthodox Christianity may have hit on the truth. We have treated the claim seriously, therefore, and have asked our readers to examine the biblical evidence for themselves.

Finally, we should like to say something about the joint authorship of this book. Each chapter was written by one of the authors and subsequently checked and approved by the other. Readers will notice differences in presentation.

We are most grateful to the readers to whom our publishers submitted our manuscript and for the helpful suggestions they made. We are especially grateful to members of the sects examined in this book who have been willing to discuss their faith with us. We respect their sincerity, even when we have been led to believe that they are sincerely wrong.

Maurice Burrell
Norwich

J. Stafford Wright
Bristol

1 The Faith and the faiths

Even before he starts on a book of this sort, the reader will have a number of questions which he hopes to find answered. They may concern specific 'faiths', or they may be more general and fundamental questions about the very *raison d'être* of such a book. Before considering the more specific issues, therefore, this chapter will be concerned with the relationship of the Faith, as an orthodox Christian sees it, and the other faiths.

Why is a discussion of these different 'insights' necessary? Surely it is a Christian duty to be tolerant, and, if people want to enjoy some variant religion, why should Christians be jealous? By what right can any religion honestly claim to be the final truth? And anyway, what do you call true Christian religion?

At first sight this book may appear to be making a lot of fuss about nothing. But it has been written in the conviction that religious beliefs are not just optional extras; they are an integral part of any faith. True Christian faith claims to rest on revelation from God, and is vital for that real quality of life which the Bible speaks of as *eternal life*, or sometimes simply as *life*. Other faiths may claim further revelations from God, and, when we encounter them, we shall naturally need to weigh them up fairly.

True Christianity

There are three important aspects of the Christian religion. The first centres in the revelation which God has made of himself and of his relationship to man. The Christian finds this in the Bible. From the Bible one gathers some understanding of God as personal and as Trinity; of Jesus Christ as God becoming fully man, and dying as the sacrifice for the sins of the world; of his genuine resurrection, his return to the heavenly sphere, and of his future return. Taken together, these beliefs form a consistent whole, and have brought illumination and new confidence to thousands upon thousands of people.

Secondly, this illumination and hope have not come through the adoption of these truths simply as a system of belief. The system is there, but, if it is true, it can become dynamic only if it is absorbed as a reality to be acted upon. 'Christ Jesus came into the world to save sinners' remains a beautiful theory until I suddenly realize 'That means me'. Then I can see that the fact demands response, and I trust him as my Saviour. So the New Testament knows two aspects of faith. There is faith in the truth of the facts and their interpretation, and there is personal trust, or committal, to the One who is the centre of these facts.

Thirdly, there is a way of life which follows on these two aspects of faith. In general the Christian naturally aims to be free of the sins for which he has been forgiven through the sacrifice of Jesus Christ. Positively he aims to be inwardly transformed to a life that is after the pattern of Christ's life. He looks for more than merely outward conformity, and for this he finds that the Holy Spirit has come in at a deep level to effect this transformation. The Holy Spirit is God in action. Yet nothing happens mechanically. We are not puppets. In Romans 12:1–2 the Christian is told to present his body as a living sacrifice to God, and, by not adopting the world's standards of thinking, to be transformed by the renewal of his mind; and many passages in the epistles urge him both to put off the bad and to put on the good (*e.g.* Ephesians 4:17–32).

It is to the credit of Christianity that so many people identify it with morality. That is one difficulty of a book like this. If one says that So-and-so is not a Christian, the average man thinks that one is accusing him of being bad and immoral. There is no surer way of producing a crop of angry letters in the papers! The point about *Christian* morality is that it is *human* morality. God did not invent a special code for Christians. He made mankind in such a way that 'right' uplifts him and makes him mature, while 'wrong' degrades both the individual and society. Thus through trial and error, through Christian and non-Christian experience, true codes of morals have emerged. These codes provide a sense of fulfilment, and go along with the aims of Christian morality.

But they go together only for a certain way. Christians do not need to contradict them, but they need to pass beyond them. Thus a code which regards man as no more than a developed animal is obviously incomplete. A code which brings in the aesthetic side will go further, and will make the man-ape see that it is 'right' to throw his banana skin into a litter bin. But until we have the right understanding of man as having a spiritual relationship with God, we still have an unsatisfied and unsatisfying morality.

So we may say that there are three pillars of genuine Christianity, and of these we are treating the first, doctrinal faith, as being of prime importance. By itself it can be dead dogma; one of the sad features of Christianity down the ages is that people have zealously recited and fought for the creeds without ever absorbing them and passing to personal trust in Jesus Christ as Saviour and Lord. On the other hand there have been attempts at inner experiences, Christian or non-Christian, in which revelatory facts have been by-passed, or indeed rejected. These have only the stability of the inner world of the experimenter himself; they are wholly subjective.

Modern mystic and meditational movements are a case in point. Many are drawn from eastern religions, which have developed some useful methods of quietening the mind. Left to themselves as subjective experiences, these methods produce a concept of pantheism, or near-pantheism. That is to say, there is developed a sense of oneness with the life of the universe, which may or may not be equated with a divine force. Christian mysticism, on the other hand, having, as it believes, God's revelation to guide it, enjoys the sense of union with God, but knows that this is not in any sense identity with him nor the outburst of inner depths of the mind, but that it is the enjoyment of fellowship with God who has shown himself to be personal.

Doctrines from the Bible

We do not propose to argue here for the Bible as being the true revelation of God. We will say only that Christians have treated it as this from the beginning. We have already indicated that the type of proof that one can offer is that it presents a consistent pattern which makes sense, and that it has opened up the transformation of lives among all strata of society and civilizations. Many would accept this but would want to make a difference between the Jesus of the Bible and the Jesus of the churches; they would maintain that the first faith was simple, but Christian dogmatists have built up a philosophy of Jesus which they have turned into an article of faith. It is important to realize that this is not so.

The Bible is not a book of nicely arranged dogmas, any more than everything in nature is in neat scientific categories. A scientist takes what he finds in nature, and deduces formulae that will make valid starting-points for anyone who wishes to understand the phenomena of the world. Similarly early Christian thinkers worked carefully through the Bible, gathered together the various events, interpretations and statements about God and man, and expressed these in those formulae that we know as the creeds and definitions. Although God has revealed truths about himself so that we may respond to him and know him, and although man is made in the likeness of God so that he can have a sensible understanding such as belongs to person with person, God inevitably surpasses man's comprehension. Thus the formulae about the Being of God and the divine-human personality of Jesus Christ were hard to fix, whereas the facts of the virgin birth and the resurrection could be stated quite simply as historical and meaningful events.

The early church records show that there were plenty of ideas about Jesus Christ that were based on one or two texts taken in isolation, just as it is possible to maintain a flat-earth theory by observing a few things and ignoring many more. Serious Christian thinkers were concerned to reach the formulae that would take account of every single statement in Scripture. From their study they concluded that God is personal and one, but that his personal Being is expressed in three 'centres'. To amplify this, while we may observe the actions of one 'centre' in, for example, the ministry of the incarnate Son, that 'centre' or Person of the Trinity is not separated from the other 'centres', the Father and the Holy Spirit. No more is the Holy Spirit, whom we now see working in the Christian church, alien from the Father and Jesus Christ. For a fuller account of the doctrine of God as Trinity, which is a major point of attack from heterodox and non-Christian faiths, the reader is referred to the appendix of this book.

Christian thinkers also tried to express the nature of Jesus Christ when he was on earth. Using the language and thought-forms of the day, they concluded that the best summary of the Bible evidence was that in Jesus Christ there were two Natures, divine and human, but he was a single Person. Thus they did justice to the New Testament statements that God became man, and to the fact that Jesus Christ appears as a single Person, not a freak split personality. (An analogy, which the early fathers did not use and which is no more than a pointer to the truth, is that all human beings are genetically two, from father and mother, but certainly are single individuals.)

Christian agreement on doctrines

Now comes an important point. These definitions were accepted by all the mainstream Christian churches, even when they became divided into sections and denominations. Such minor differences as, for example, whether the Holy Spirit proceeds from the Father and the Son, or from the Father only, are neither here nor there. The significant thing is that, even after the major rift of the Reformation, Protestants and Roman Catholics and the Eastern Orthodox accepted the creeds and definitions as true statements, inasmuch as they could be proved from the Bible.

So, if Christians are attacked for making the Bible say anything they choose, they can say that on the fundamentals of the Being of God and the Person and work of Jesus Christ the churches agree that the orthodox creeds and definitions summarize what the Bible says. Many theologians today want to change the definitions, not simply to express them in modern terms as we have tried to do in this chapter; but in making the changes, they admittedly have to part company with the New Testament as a whole.

In this book we shall be concerned with several sects which profess to accept what the Bible says but which hold that the Christian church has been wrong in its formulae. This at once raises a difficult point, because, if they are right, then God has allowed the whole church to be in error over vital matters all down the centuries, until some person in the 19th or 20th century suddenly discovered the truth. If these founders of modern religions agreed on what the Bible says about these vital facts, we might take notice. But in fact they all differ. Hence it is a useful practice for a Christian student to study the evidence for the orthodox formulae, comparing Scripture with Scripture. This is what we have attempted to do in the appendix on the doctrine of the Trinity.

We have already mentioned the obvious fact that there are a number of Christian denominations which disagree over Christian truths. It is perfectly possible to disagree over a number of points, such as the nature of the ministry, the organization of the local church, the significance of the sacraments and the manner of their administration, without losing hold of the great Christian verities. The faiths with which we deal in this book go far beyond this. While the mainstream Christian churches are making serious efforts to work together, these other faiths have no desire at all to join with others, nor would it be possible to work with them because of their abandonment of the doctrinal grounds on which true Christianity stands.

From time to time one finds that these other faiths hold views which are held at least by some smaller groups of orthodox Christians. Where this is so, we have not gone out of our way to argue against such views, even though we cannot agree with the way in which they are promoted as vital. For example, Calvinism and Arminianism both find a legitimate place among Christians, and we should not criticize a sect for Arminianism unless this has been developed into a doctrine of justification by works. Similarly there is room for varying interpretations of the millennial reign of Christ.

Perhaps the most debatable doctrine which we have refrained from criticizing is that of conditional immortality, held by Jehovah's Witnesses and Christadelphians. This belief is that a human being has no inherent immortality, but that eternal life is the gift of God for those who are to be saved. The lost, according to this view, will cease to exist after the final judgment, and the punishment of this second death will be eternal in the sense that it will never be revoked. Once again, there are many orthodox Christians who hold this view as a legitimate interpretation of scriptural statements. It is not the same as universalism, which says that everyone will ultimately be saved.

These movements accept it in the form of soul sleep, which is equivalent to non-existence between death and the resurrection; i.e. there can be no such being as a bodiless man. Some orthodox Christians also take this view, but others accept a bodiless existence of a person after death, in the traditional manner. After the final judgment they hold that the unsaved will be blotted out.

It may be asked why these deviant faiths arise. The reasons are complex. Obviously they appeal to an inner need of some people, who do not see that this need may be more truly met in the Christian faith. Often the church is at fault. People need authority and need clear truth. If preaching and teaching are at a low ebb and the pulpit is merely a sounding-board for moral platitudes, then the dogmatic agent at the door, with his 'This is what the Bible says', will always capture the hungry sheep. Or if the church becomes more of a business concerned with getting things done and forgets the quiet times of devotion and meditation which answer the deep spiritual needs of men, then the movements that offer inner experiences will flourish. These are two extreme situations; but no amount of examples will explain everything, any more than one can explain why people become atheists. What we can see, however, is that if a person gravitates into one of the faiths, he will choose one of his own type, to fit his own inner world. To take two more extreme cases, it would be quite impossible for a Jehovah's Witness ever to have become a Theosophist.

In studying the faiths described in this book, it will be

13

found that some make use of old ideas which were rejected by the early fathers. Thus Jehovah's Witnesses adopt the idea of Arius in the fourth century that the Son is not God from all eternity, but was the first created being. Christadelphians and Anthroposophists reintroduce something like the early ideas of Adoptionism, that the man, Jesus, was adopted by the Father when the Christ descended on him at his baptism. But many of the ideas are new.

Seventh-Day Adventism

Finally we need to explain why, unlike the previous editions of this book, this new one contains no separate chapter about Seventh-Day Adventism. The reason is simply that, unlike the deviant sects which follow, Seventh-Day Adventists accept the full Christian belief in the Trinity and in the deity and incarnation of Christ, his atoning death on the cross, and his resurrection and ascension. In a few less important areas of belief and practice their biblical interpretations are unusual, however, and it may be helpful to readers if we draw attention to one of these, while at the same time pointing out that, in the main, they stand where orthodox Christianity stands. We have chosen sabbath-observance, for, as their name indicates, one of their chief differences from other Christians is their view that all Christians should continue to observe the Jewish sabbath rather than the Christian Sunday.

The standard Christian belief is that during New Testament times Christians came to observe the first day of the week, in memory of Christ's resurrection, and gradually ceased to observe the Saturday sabbath. The New Testament makes it clear, for example, that on the first day of the week the disciples gathered to break bread (Acts 20:7), that one of their priorities on that day was to set aside their offerings for God's work (1 Corinthians 16:2), and that John was 'in the Spirit on the Lord's day' when he was commanded to write down his revelation (Revelation 1:10). It is interesting to note that in this last passage the Greek does not say 'the day of the Lord', but uses an adjective with the general meaning of 'belonging to the Lord'. Its only other occurrence in Scripture is in 1 Corinthians 11:20, 'the Lord's supper'. This expression, 'the Lord's day', is used of the first day of the week soon after New Testament times. Thus Ignatius in his Letter to the Magnesians 9:1 speaks of Christians as 'no longer observing sabbaths, but fashioning their lives after the Lord's day on which our life also rose through him'. The so-called Epistle of Barnabas, early in post-apostolic times, speaks of keeping 'the eighth day with joyfulness, the day on which Jesus rose from the dead' (15:9). Justin Martyr in the middle of the second century mentions the gathering of Christians on Sunday (Apology 1:67). There are several similar references which show that the first day was the regular day of Christian observance long before any Council decreed it. These are the indications on which the orthodox Christian rests. The first day was certainly observed soon after the New Testament was written; therefore we look for anything in the New Testament that would show that it was observed before the canon of Scripture was closed, and, as we have seen, the verses are there.

With this in mind we look at the Adventist case. We may dismiss as irrelevant the fact that Jesus Christ kept the sabbath, since this was before his resurrection. Similarly the visits of Paul and others to the synagogues on the sabbath were not for Christian worship, but to take advantage of the services in order to preach the gospel to the Jews. We are left with the strong argument that the sabbath is incorporated in the Ten Commandments, and, if we observe the rest of the commandments, we have no right to change this one. However, the New Testament does not agree. It quotes other commands from the Decalogue (Mark 10:19; Romans 13:8–10), but never the one on the sabbath. It goes further, and in Colossians 2:16–17 Paul says that no-one is to judge the Christian on matters of food and drink, or with regard to a festival or a new moon or a sabbath. This can only mean that the sabbath is no longer a normal part of the Christian calendar. Although Galatians 4:10 mentions 'days, and months, and seasons, and years' in general terms, it is likely that Paul included the Saturday sabbath here also.

The Adventist answer is that the reference in Colossians 2 is to the seven extra rest days that formed part of the festivals (e.g. Leviticus 23:32). One would reply that it is absolutely impossible for a Hebrew like Paul to speak of sabbaths if he meant only seven days in the year and excluded the weekly sabbath. This would be even more so if he is writing to Gentiles, who certainly would know what the weekly sabbath was, but who would have little idea of the technical extra sabbaths of the law. We note also that Colossians 2:16–17 links together the new moon and the sabbath, as is often done in the Old Testament, where there is no doubt that the weekly sabbath is referred to, the new moon being the regular first day of the month festival (*e.g.* Isaiah 1:13). Paul declares that the sabbath is a shadow, which is fulfilled in Christ (Colossians 2:17). Two reasons are given in the law for observing the sabbath. In Exodus 20:11 it is in memory of God's completion of creation. In Deuteronomy 5:15 it is in memory of redemption from Egypt. These were shadows of the new creation and the full redemption that have come through Christ's death on the cross and its culmination in his resurrection on the first day.

It is right to point out that nowadays the Adventists do not say that sabbath-keeping is necessary for salvation, nor that worshippers on Sunday have the mark of the beast upon them. They say that they observe the sabbath out of loyalty to the expressed will of God. Needless to say, in rejecting the seventh day as the proper day for Christians to observe, we do not reject the principle of setting apart the first day as the Lord's day for worship, service and rest. Experience has proved the value of God's creation ordinance in this respect.

For further reading

Those readers wishing to explore the beliefs and practices of Seventh-Day Adventists in more depth might like to know that the Adventists have published a reasoned account of themselves in a substantial book called *Questions on Doctrine* (1957). An assessment that is critical and yet more favourable than some other Christian works is that of Walter R. Martin, *The Truth About Seventh-Day Adventism* (Marshall, Morgan and Scott, 1960). Martin was answered by Norman F. Douty in *Another Look at Seventh-Day Adventism* (Marshall, Morgan and Scott, 1962). A more recent book by an Anglican, Geoffrey

Paxton, *The Shaking of Adventism* (Zenith, 1981) shows that there remains a division within the movement about the relation between justification and sanctification. Paxton argues that the outcome of their struggle will decide whether Seventh-Day Adventists will move closer to mainstream Christianity or further from it.

2 Jehovah's Witnesses

Jehovah's Witnesses are the most active proselytizers of all the established religious sects. Every Witness is regarded as a missionary, a publisher of the sect's message and a distributor of its literature. No-one is recognized as a Jehovah's Witness until he is engaging in such activities in an allotted area and obediently returning records of his work to the Kingdom Hall, his local headquarters and meeting-place. From the sect's President to its rawest recruit, all are expected to achieve a monthly quota of door-to-door visits. They run the risk of severe rebuke if they fail to live up to expectations.

The ordinary Witness, who does a full-time secular job and performs his religious duties in his spare time, is expected to spend ten hours engaged in such visiting each month. The 'pioneer', the Witness who takes a part-time job so that he may be free to give more of his time to these missionary activities, devotes a hundred hours a month to visiting. The 'special pioneer', who works full-time for the organization in return for a modest wage, is asked to fulfil a monthly quota of 140 hours.

Several factors help to explain the Witnesses' zeal in such missionary outreach. There is the natural desire to fulfil the expectations of their leaders, coupled with the incentive to be at least as good as their fellow-Witnesses in achieving the required standard. There are also theological incentives. In common with most of the sects, Jehovah's Witnesses believe that they alone possess God's message for the world's salvation. This is allied with the belief that the battle of Armageddon and the end of the present world is imminent and that the only hope for survival lies in becoming Jehovah's Witnesses. Most members also appear to believe that their own individual salvation depends to some extent on their fulfilment of this task. So in almost all towns and villages, all the year round, but especially on Saturdays and Sundays, Jehovah's Witnesses of all ages can be seen busily working their particular patches.

A brief history

The history of Jehovah's Witnesses begins with the birth of Charles Taze Russell on 16 February 1852 in Pittsburgh, Pennsylvania. After his mother died when he was nine, Russell developed a close relationship with his father and later joined him in his clothing business. As a young man, he attended orthodox Christian churches and joined the Young Men's Christian Association. With evangelistic zeal he used to chalk texts on walls so that passing workmen might be challenged with the need to repent. Soon, however, Russell began to have serious doubts about the Christian faith and was at the point of giving up Christianity completely when a sermon by an Adventist preacher, Jonas Wendell, convinced him of the divine inspiration and authority of the Bible. From that day onwards, Russell was an ardent Bible student.

Claiming to approach the Scriptures without any preconceived ideas, Russell decided that many of the tenets of orthodox Christianity ought to be rejected as unscriptural. He also came to believe that a literal second coming of Christ was imminent. Before long, however, he was teaching that Christ's return would be invisible, an idea which he publicized in a pamphlet, *The Object and Manner of the Lord's Return.*

By 1876 the twenty-four-year-old Russell had gathered around him about thirty disciples. He then met N. H. Barbour, author of a magazine called *The Herald of the Morning,* with whose views he was pleased to discover he had much in common. For a time the two men joined forces, Russell becoming co-editor of Barbour's magazine. Russell had already given up his clothing business to devote his life to full-time preaching. He used to travel from city to city, preaching on weekdays in the open air and on Sundays in

Protestant churches. He and Barbour wrote *Three Worlds or Plan of Redemption*, arguing that Christ's Second Presence, as they were now calling it, had begun in the autumn of 1874. They went on to claim that, just as at his first coming Jesus had preached for three-and-a-half years (from the baptism to the crucifixion), so his Second Presence would be of similar duration. This meant that God's Kingdom would be set up in 1878 and that the saints on earth would then be carried away into heaven. Anticipating that event, some of their followers dressed in white robes and assembled to await their expected rapture. Subsequent disillusionment led them to forsake Russell and Barbour. Russell, however, merely went back to his study of the Bible, concluding that the mistake was one of misinterpretation and miscalculation. As we shall see, such an attitude has been characteristic of Jehovah's Witness eschatology ever since, the most recent example being in 1975 when most Witnesses were expecting the battle of Armageddon.

Following doctrinal disagreements, Russell and Barbour parted company. Russell then started his own magazine, *The Watch Tower and Herald of Christ's Presence*, the first edition of which appeared on 1 July 1879 with 6,000 copies. Twenty-five years later the circulation had grown to 25,000. Now known by the shorter name *The Watchtower*, it has a circulation of about ten million each fortnightly issue and appears in more than eighty languages. It has always been recognized as the sect's official mouthpiece.

Within a year of the magazine's appearance, Russell's growing number of supporters were organized in thirty congregations in Pennsylvania and the surrounding states. They found their unity, not through the elaborate bureaucratic structure which developed later, but in a common informal acceptance of Russell's leadership and in a willingness to follow the patterns set by the Pittsburgh congregation, where Russell himself was a member.

These early Russellites, as they were dubbed (for the name Jehovah's Witnesses was given to them much later by J. F. Rutherford), busied themselves in producing and distributing many tracts, their stated aim being to 'expose fallacies of church doctrines'. To help to achieve this aim, Russell established Zion's Watch Tower Tract Society in 1881. Three years later this became the Watch Tower Tract Society, with seven directors, including a president (Russell himself), a vice-president, and a secretary-treasurer. There was a further change of name in 1896 to the present Watch Tower Bible and Tract Society, but the earlier structure has remained. The sect is still controlled by a powerful triumvirate backed by four other directors.

The number of Russell's followers increased steadily as the years went by, largely because of his own ceaseless activities. After the success of *The Watchtower* he produced many other books, including his series of *Studies in the Scriptures,* which set out clearly his own distinctive and heretical views but which his followers claimed were indispensable for a true understanding of the Bible. He also travelled widely, preaching, lecturing and promoting his writings. He visited Great Britain in 1891, 1903, 1907 and 1910; the London branch office was opened in 1900, and the International Bible Students' Association, an offshoot of the American Watch Tower Society, was established in Britain in 1914.

After the 1878 disappointment, Russell had gone on to predict that the Christ who had returned invisibly in 1874 would take the elect into God's Kingdom in 1914. Excitement mounted among the Russellites as the year approached and the feverish work of preparing people for the expected end continued unabated. Millions of publications were distributed and Russell's sermons were syndicated in newspapers in North America and Europe. Membership grew in many parts of the world. But Russell himself became less explicit as 1914 drew nearer, even though many of his followers continued to make extravagant claims which brought ridicule upon themselves and the movement. By 1914, however, there were 1,200 congregations linked together under Russell's leadership, with a total membership of some 15,000 active followers and about 55,000 regular subscribers to *The Watchtower.* Nevertheless the year brought another disappointment when the promise of rapture was not fulfilled. As it happened, Russell's own end was not long delayed, for on 31 October 1916 he died in Texas on the way home from a preaching tour.

After a brief but bitter struggle for power, J. F. Rutherford emerged as the sect's new leader. Born in Missouri on 8 November 1869, he became a lawyer with a very successful practice and eventually was made a circuit judge in his home state. He came into contact with Russell's teaching in 1894 through the work of a door-to-door visitor, but was not baptized until 1906. His rise within the movement was rapid. He became Russell's legal adviser in 1907 and worked at the Pittsburgh headquarters. As Russell's health began to decline, Rutherford came into prominence as an able speaker, some-times substituting for his sick leader. Ten years after his baptism he became the sect's leader.

His style of leadership was very different from the gentler Russell's and this led to inevitable conflict with those who had worked closely with the founder. Rutherford, however, proved more than a match for his opponents. A few disaffected members formed small, breakaway groups, some of which persisted, but Rutherford took most of the membership with him and more than made up for the deserters by the number of new converts. From Russell he inherited about 16,000 members: he handed over to his successor more than 100,000.

It is instructive to notice the steps he took to ensure his personal control over every aspect of the movement's activi-ties, not only because of what they reveal about his own character, but also because they focus attention on some of the characteristics still found in the contemporary movement.

Rutherford's overall aim was to dominate the sect's rather loose organization, to rid it of all democratic elements, and to transform it into a tightly-knit bureaucratic structure over which he would reign supreme. He rationalized his own megalomania by explaining that democracy was to give way to theocracy, human control to divine control. So when the Society spoke, members were to hear Jehovah speaking: and for all practical purposes Rutherford was the Society.

He began, therefore, by using all the expertise of his legal training and experience to manipulate the Society's rules in order to rid himself of those directors who were not willing to back him. He then dismissed all members of the headquarters staff who had sympathized with the views of the sacked directors. Next he turned his attention to the congregations which, as we have seen, had been linked together in a loose federation of those loyal to Russell's leadership. In place of democratically elected elders leading these congregations, he insisted that the most important work, that of door-to-door outreach and literature distribution, must be placed under the direct control of service directors whom he appointed in each congregation. By 1932 these service directors had completely ousted the former elders and had absolute control of the congregations. Six years later, the last vestiges of democracy were completely removed and Rutherford had insisted that all holding office in the congregations were to be appointed by the Society. Earlier he had introduced the zone system, with a number of congregations being grouped together in a geographical area and all accountable to a zone servant, who was himself accountable to Rutherford. In such ways, therefore, Rutherford had succeeded in imposing his own bureaucratic structure upon Jehovah's Witnesses, and over it all he himself had almost absolute power.

One of the problems Rutherford faced early on in his leadership was the undoubted posthumous influence that Russell still enjoyed within the movement. At his death *The Watchtower* had said that, next to Paul, he was the greatest man who ever lived. His books, as we have seen, were regarded as indispensable for a correct interpretation of the Bible and were often valued more highly than the Bible itself. Rutherford's response to such a situation was gradually to replace all Russell's books with his own. Thus publications like *The Harp of God, Jehovah, Creation* and *Life* ensured that Rutherford, rather than his predecessor, became the sect's arbiter in all matters of faith and conduct.

The importance he attached to doctrinal uniformity can be seen from the fact that in 1922 he ordered that, in future, study of *The Watchtower* should take place in groups, as well as individually, and that the members of the groups should answer printed questions on the magazine's articles to ensure that they had imbibed its teaching. Such uniformity of belief led also to uniformity of presentation of the sect's teachings to others, for Rutherford's monthly *Bulletin* contained talks and testimonies for members to learn by heart before passing them on to contacts.

The fact that members took the sect's doctrinal pronouncements so seriously led to trouble in 1925. We noted earlier the problems raised under Russell's leadership by the sect's tendency to fix on certain dates as the time of the rapture. Under Rutherford's influence, members had now been encouraged to think of 1925 as the correct date. However, when that year also came and went without the fulfilment of expectations, there was another spate of desertions by disillusioned members. A much more significant feature of that year, however, was the prominence that now came to be given to Jehovah as the proper name for God. In 1931 Rutherford took the decisive step of renaming his followers Jehovah's Witnesses, thus bringing to an end the confusion which had resulted from the various other names by which they had been known.

Rutherford died on 8 January 1942, after an illness which had made him increasingly less active in the movement's affairs. He was succeeded by Nathan H. Knorr, who was born in Bethlehem, Pennsylvania in 1905. After being brought up in orthodox Christian circles, Knorr became a Jehovah's Witness when he was sixteen, a full-time worker for the sect at eighteen, and a member of the Watch Tower Society's headquarters staff soon afterwards. His extraordinary organizing gifts were quickly recognized and by 1932 he had become general manager of the Watch Tower publishing office and printing plant. Two years later he was appointed a director of the Society and in 1940 became its vice-president. He was in a key position during Rutherford's declining years, therefore, and as his predecessor became more of a recluse Knorr found himself with ever-increasing responsibilities for the day-to-day running of the Society's affairs. Five days after Rutherford's death he received the unanimous support of his six fellow-directors and became president.

The personality of the president has been much less in evidence since Rutherford's death. Russell had been a cult figure loved by most members of the sect. Rutherford had stated his determination to play down the cult of personality, but his own egocentric nature made this impossible. Although Knorr lacked the personal appeal of his predecessors, he nevertheless proved to be a very effective leader of a different kind, playing the part of chief executive over an ever-increasingly bureaucratic organization. The thirty-five years of his presidency witnessed a more rapid growth of membership and world-wide impact than the sect had ever enjoyed before. Most of the credit for such advances must go to Knorr; they were largely the result of the training methods he encouraged every congregation to adopt, for through such methods members became more effective proselytizers. When Knorr died in the summer of 1977, he was succeeded by his vice-president, F. W. Franz, who for many years has been the chief writer of the sect's books on doctrine.

It is difficult to give accurate membership figures, for although the sect publishes an annual *Yearbook* containing many statistics, actual membership figures are not included. If, however, we take the movement's point that to be recognized as an active Jehovah's Witness one must be engaging in door-to-door work and distributing the sect's publications, then helpful figures are available. According to the 1980 *Yearbook* the peak number of 'publishers', as such active workers are described, was 2,186,075 working in 205 countries. There were some 77,634 'publishers' at work in the British Isles. These figures seem rather low for a sect which once claimed to be the fastest growing religion in the world, but perhaps a more realistic assessment of the strength of Jehovah's Witnesses world-wide and in the British Isles is provided by the attendance figures for the sect's annual Memorial, when members meet to remember the death of Jesus. The 1980 *Yearbook* states that 5,323,766 attended the Memorial world-wide, 158,167 of them in the British Isles. In round figures, therefore, there are probably about six million Jehovah's Witnesses in the world and less than 160,000 in the British Isles. About half the British Isles members seem to be active in regular door-to-door outreach.

What they believe

Authority

Jehovah's Witnesses claim that their beliefs are derived directly from the Bible, which, they say, they accept as the authoritative Word of God. Their publications ask readers to 'study according to what God Himself has to say in His own Word', claiming 'our appeal is to the Bible for truth'.[1] A Watch Tower publication argues, 'The Bible is the truth, God's Word. If we follow it faithfully we shall not be misled... The Holy Bible can be proved to be the one sacred book of divine truth.'[2] One of their chief criticisms of mainstream Christianity, from the days of Russell to the present time, is that the churches have all departed from the plain teachings of the Bible, replacing them with their own man-made and demon-inspired religious dogma.

Despite their claim to be a *Bible-only* group, however, the Witnesses turn out to be a *Bible-plus* group, their *plus* being in the form of their Watch Tower publications. Individual Witnesses are never encouraged to read the Bible with an open mind and to draw their own conclusions, but are expected to accept without question what the sect's publications tell them to believe. There is no room for the slightest disagreement on the smallest points.

This quickly becomes obvious to anyone attempting to discuss the Bible's teaching with Jehovah's Witnesses. Every Witness will produce the same answer, almost parrot-fashion. They are like puppets performing the required antics when the strings are pulled. Having been taught not to think independently, they simply repeat (often word for word) what they have gleaned from their study of Watch Tower books in their training sessions. Ex-Witnesses, like Ted Dencher and William Schnell, make the point that as Witnesses they were expected to reproduce the Watch Tower interpretations of the Bible without question.

The sect's justification for this practice is based on a peculiar interpretation of Matthew 24:45, 'Who is the trusty servant, the sensible man charged by his master to manage his household staff and issue their rations at the proper time?' The Witnesses' answer to the Lord's question is that 'the trusty servant', or in their own jargon 'the discreet slave class', are a small but élite group of Witnesses from whom the main body of rank-and-file Witnesses obtain their spiritual food, that is the one and only correct interpretation of the Bible. Thus whatever is passed down from the sect's Brooklyn headquarters, by way of the fortnightly *Watchtower* magazine or other publications, is received by all Jehovah's Witnesses throughout the world as Jehovah's truth.

Interpretations of scriptural passages passed down to members in this way usually illustrate how adept this 'discreet slave class' is at mishandling Scripture to prove its own points. Texts are often taken out of context and Watch Tower dogmas are read back into them. A flagrant example is the way the sect's leaders misuse verses like Leviticus 3:17; 7:26f. and 17:10–14 in a forlorn attempt to find a biblical basis for their objection to blood transfusions. From such verses they claim that anyone who willingly allows himself or his dependents to receive blood runs the risk of forfeiting eternal life for himself and them. Studied in context, however, these passages say nothing about blood transfusions, but set out the Mosaic law banning the drinking of the blood of animals. Other examples of the misuse of Scripture will be seen when later we examine specific Watch Tower doctrines.

Although Jehovah's Witnesses are allowed to use any version of the Bible, preference is given to their own *New World Translation*. The sect claims that, unlike all other translations, this one is not coloured in any way by the doctrinal presuppositions of those responsible for it, but is as accurate as consecrated powers make possible. In fact, almost the exact opposite is true. At many points the *New World Translation* mistranslates the text in such a way as to obscure the plain meaning of the original and to support specific Jehovah's Witness doctrines.

In practice, despite the lip-service paid to the Bible's authority, the Scriptures are studied hardly at all. Whereas mainstream Christianity uses the Bible as a yardstick against which to judge the teachings and practices of the churches, among Jehovah's Witnesses the voice of the sect's leadership, as expressed pre-eminently in *The Watchtower,* is the only legitimate key to an understanding of the Bible. Thus Bible passages are always approached through Watch Tower publications, and what are called Bible study groups are in reality studies of the sect's literature.

Jesus Christ

On the authority of the Bible, Christians believe that Jesus

Christ is both God and man. The first disciples knew Jesus as a real human being, living and working among them. As time passed, however, and their experience of him deepened, they were compelled to acknowledge that, although he was truly human, he was not merely human. His life, his claims, his miracles, and finally the vindication of his resurrection led them to recognize that in dealing with him they were dealing with God. Thomas was speaking for them all when he confessed, 'My Lord and my God!' (John 20:28). What is more, Jesus accepted this as a true estimate of his person.

The writer of the Fourth Gospel appears to have had no doubts about Christ's deity. His opening words state, 'When all things began, the Word already was. The Word dwelt with God, and what God was, the Word was.' In contrast, Jehovah's Witnesses deny Christ's essential deity. Although they are prepared to speak of him as divine, they refuse to acknowledge him as God in the full sense of that word. So they maintain that whereas Christ is 'a god' (with a small g), the Father is 'the God' (with a capital G). Thus Christ is regarded as a secondary or demi-god. To maintain this view, which so obviously conflicts with the clear teaching of John 1:1, the Watch Tower authorities have mistranslated that verse as follows: 'Originally the Word was, and the Word was with God, and the Word was a god.'[3] There is no justification for such a translation in the Greek text:[4] the verse does not allow us to distinguish between the kind of Godhood Christ enjoys and the kind of Godhood the Father has. As a distinguished New Testament scholar has written, 'The divinity that belongs to the rest of the Godhead belongs also to Him.'[5] In other words, John 1:1 means what Christians have always believed it to mean, that Christ is God in every sense of the word – 'what God was, the Word was'.

Because Christians believe in the deity of Christ, they also recognize his eternity. Christ is God, and God is eternal: therefore Christ is eternal. There has never been a time when the Son did not exist as the eternal Son of God. Jehovah's Witnesses reject this view. They are prepared to say that Christ had an existence prior to his birth at Bethlehem, but because they recognize only the Father (or Jehovah, as they prefer to call him) as fully God, they do not believe that

Christ has existed eternally. In other words, they believe in Christ's pre-existence but deny his eternity, maintaining that there was a time when Jehovah-God was all alone in universal space. When Jehovah began to create, they claim, his first creative act was his Son.

They claim to find biblical evidence for this belief mainly in two verses, Colossians 1:15, where Christ is described as 'the first-born of all creation', and Revelation 3:14, where he is called 'the beginning of God's creation'. When we examine these verses more carefully, however, it becomes clear that they do not support the Witness view.

In Colossians 1:15 the Greek for 'first-born' is *prōtotokos*, which can mean 'the first' and 'the chief' as well as 'the first-born'. It certainly does not mean 'the first-created', as Jehovah's Witnesses allege: that meaning would require a word like *prōtoktistos*. In any case, the context shows clearly that the main point at issue is Christ's superiority over creation, not his relationship to the Father. What Paul means is that Christ is supreme over creation and heir of all things.

Turning to Revelation 3:14, everything depends on what is meant by 'the beginning'. Disagreeing with the Jehovah's Witness claim that it shows that Christ was God's first creative act and that Christ is, therefore, a creature, Christians believe it means that Christ is *the one through whom the creative work was done*. Christ is described as 'the beginning of God's creation', therefore, because he began it. That the word 'the beginning' need not be interpreted in the Jehovah's Witness way is clearly indicated in Revelation 21:6, where God himself is described as 'the beginning'. And not even Jehovah's Witnesses would claim that this means that God was the first one to be created!

Colossians 1:15 and Revelation 3:14 support the orthodox Christian view of Christ's eternity, rather than the Witness view of Christ's creatureliness. The translators of the New English Bible were fully justified, therefore, in rendering the two verses, 'his is the primacy over all created things' and he is 'the prime source of all God's creation'. The Good News Bible is even clearer: 'Christ is...superior to all created things' and is 'the origin of all that God has created'.

So Christians believe that by a miraculous act of God the

child born to Mary was both God and man (Luke 1:35; 2:11; Galatians 4:4; *etc.*). He was not only God, nor was he merely man; he was and is a unique Person, God and man. So, on the one hand, the writer to the Hebrews could say that Jesus 'in every respect has been tempted as we are' (4:15) because of his humanity, and, on the other, Thomas could confess, 'My Lord and my God!' (John 20:28) because of Christ's deity.

Jehovah's Witnesses completely repudiate this idea of incarnation, as understood by Christians. Instead, they maintain that the life-force of the pre-existent son was transferred from heaven to the womb of the virgin Mary. The result was that Jesus was born as a man, no more and no less. Not content with this rejection of Christian doctrine, they often mis-state the Christian view and then ridicule their own mis-statements of it. Russell, for example, claimed that Christians believed Jesus assumed a human body by a kind of materialization such as that of the angels who appeared to Abraham in Genesis 18. Rutherford maintained that incarnation involved the belief that Jesus was a spirit-being and that his flesh was merely a covering or house in which this spirit-being lived. A more recent Watch Tower book repeats this as 'a spirit person clothed with flesh'.[6]

It must be stated that these views are not a fair representation of the Christian doctrine of incarnation. Jehovah's Witnesses of course have the right to disagree with the Christian view if they so desire, but it is dishonest of them to misrepresent the Christian view and then condemn Christians for views which no orthodox Christians hold.

Turning from Christ's Person to his work, it is obvious to all who read the New Testament that the cross is central to all that is said about salvation. Christians are shown that they cannot earn their salvation. They, together with the rest of the human race, are sinners whom Christ died to save. They believe that, because Christ died and thus paid sin's penalty, all may be forgiven and returned to fellowship with God. Christians therefore rejoice in the New Testament assurance that, when a person puts his faith in Christ, his sins are forgiven, he is reconciled to God, he is born again and he receives God's gift of eternal life.

Jehovah's Witnesses deny these New Testament truths, teaching instead that by his death Christ has simply redeemed us from physical death and that, as we trust him and work for him now, we are assured of partaking in the resurrection hereafter. That resurrection will be to what they call life under favourable conditions, where there will be a fair test of loyalty to God. For those who successfully pass through this second probationary period there will be the reward of ever-lasting life – for the favoured few in heaven, and for the vast majority on earth. Everyone else will be annihilated. All this means that the Watch Tower way of salvation is a 'do-it-yourself' enterprise, for a person's salvation depends upon what he himself does to earn it, rather than upon what Christ has done on his behalf.

This is clearly a travesty of New Testament teaching. The Christian gospel tells us that Christ has redeemed us, not merely from physical death, but from the guilt and power of sin (Romans 3:23–28; Galatians 1:4; 3:13; 1 John 1:6–10; 3:5). Those who put their trust and confidence in him are assured of eternal life here and now (John 3:36; 5:24; Romans 6:23). They are not (as the Jehovah's Witnesses claim) called to work for eternal life under 'favourable conditions' when they have died and been raised, but to accept it as God's free gift here and now. So the New Testament states quite clearly, 'God gave us eternal life, and this life is in his Son. He who has the Son has life; he who has not the Son of God has not life' (1 John 5:11–12). The New Testament sweeps aside all human pretensions and every idea that we can earn God's favour, making it crystal clear that the only thing we can contribute to our salvation is the sin from which we need to be saved (Ephesians 2:8).

It is important to see that Jehovah's Witnesses divide Christ's existence into what amounts to three unconnected chronological phases.[7] As a pre-existent spirit being, he lived with Jehovah as the archangel Michael; after his virgin birth, he existed on earth as a mere human being, no more and no less; at his resurrection he was exalted as a divine spirit once more and thus ascended to his Father's right hand in invisible form. It is doubtful whether the sect's leaders have ever tried to think through the theological implications of this view of a three-phase Christ. At the very least, there appears to be no real connection between the three phases. At worst, they appear to be three distinct beings. On the basis of this strange Christology, however, Jehovah's Witnesses are able to deny the bodily resurrection of Jesus, claiming that God miraculously removed and hid the dead body of the human Jesus. They explain the resurrection appearances by stating that the resurrected Christ, once again a divine spirit being, materialized bodies when it suited his purpose to do this. These appearances are then explained as temporary expediencies to support the first disciples, whose faith was not yet strong enough to accept the real truth of the matter. The Witnesses go on to assert that the invisible Christ then ascended to his exalted place at his Father's right hand until in 1918, again as an invisible spirit, his second coming took place.

The New Testament story of Christ is very different. The risen Christ had a real, though transformed, body (Luke 24:37–43). When he ascended to his Father's side, our humanity was exalted with and in him; and he now stands in the presence of God on our behalf (Hebrews 9:24). One day he will return and every eye will see him (Acts 1:11; Revelation 1:7).

The Holy Spirit

As far as one can discover anything about the Spirit from Watch Tower publications, and there is a significant gap in their theology on this subject, Jehovah's Witnesses regard the Spirit as an impersonal force. One of their doctrinal handbooks defines the Spirit as 'Jehovah's invisible energising force (greater than atomic energy) that produces visible results in many manifestations experienced by men'.[8] Another book, concluding a section which has attempted to show that the doctrine of the Trinity has no biblical foundation, asserts, 'As for the holy spirit with which Jesus was anointed, this spirit is not a person at all but is God's invisible active force by means of which God carries out his holy will and work.'[9] To the Witnesses, the Spirit is always 'it' and the name is never written with capital initials.

Their view has serious implications. Rejecting the New

Testament's view of the Spirit's deity, Witnesses do not believe that every true servant of God has been born again of the Spirit (John 3:5, *etc.*), but, as we shall see later, they limit the number of the born again to an élite body of 144,000.

In contrast, Christians believe that the Spirit is not a mere influence or invisible force, but a divine Person. Accepting New Testament teaching at its face value, they believe the Spirit is the one who teaches, bears witness, convicts, guides, and can be grieved, and that he has the characteristics of a person (John 14 – 16). Christians accept the New Testament verdict that to lie to the Spirit is to lie to God (Acts 5:3f.). Above all, they rejoice in the assurance that by the work of the Spirit within them they have been born again (John 3).

The Trinity

It will now be obvious that Jehovah's Witnesses completely reject the Christian doctrine of the Trinity, believing it to be not only unscriptural but also satanic. As we have seen, they believe that the one God, Jehovah, created a Son, Jesus Christ; so this Son is god in a limited sense, god with a small 'g'. Moreover, they assert, Christians are wrong in describing 'holy spirit' as God and person, for the spirit is God's invisible active force at work in the world.

The biblical basis on which Christians hold the doctrine of the Trinity is examined in the Appendix. Here we simply note that the grounds on which Jehovah's Witnesses reject that doctrine are very similar to those which led Arius to reject it in the fourth century AD. It is not surprising to find, therefore, that Jehovah's Witnesses see in Arius the champion of a true minority view against the erroneous view of the majority of insincere clerics who, they claim, perverted the original Christian truth with their own man-made and devil-inspired dogmas. Thus we find that, whereas the Christian church pronounced Arius a heretic and, more positively, set out the commonly accepted view of Christ in what we now call the Nicene Creed, Jehovah's Witnesses agree with Arius at almost every major point.

The 144,000

Jehovah's Witnesses believe in two grades of salvation, for

144,000 in heaven, and for the remainder of the worthy on earth. Only the 'little flock', the 144,000 of the book of Revelation, will go to heaven. They alone are the twice-born, the spirit-begotten sons of God, who will reign with Christ in the heavenly Kingdom. Only those who feel sure in their hearts that they are members of this élite body actually partake of the bread and wine during the annual Memorial ceremony. On the other hand, there remains a vast crowd of 'other sheep', faithful Jehovah's Witnesses who do not expect heavenly reward but look forward to eternal life on earth.

Various questions will arise in the minds of Christians who take the trouble to read the relevant sections of the book of Revelation. Are they really justified in limiting the number in heaven to 144,000? The book of Revelation makes great use of poetic imagery and uses numbers symbolically. Moreover, in Revelation 7 the 144,000 are the 'sealed' out of 'every tribe of the sons of Israel' (verse 4). If we take this part of the chapter literally we shall refer it to the number of *Jews* in heaven. With typical inconsistency, Jehovah's Witnesses expect us to understand the number 144,000 *literally* and the 12,000 of each tribe *symbolically*. Most commentators would understand the whole passage symbolically. Some say it represents the saved under the old covenant. Others, understanding 'Israel' as the church, the true Israel of God, say it points to the complete number of the New Testament saints. In any case, it is worth noticing that in addition to the 144,000 the context mentions another great multitude 'which no man could number' who were 'standing before the throne and before the Lamb' (verse 9). Nor can anyone who has read John 10:16 in its context understand the 'other sheep' as those believers who do not expect to go to heaven, for Jesus is obviously referring to the Gentiles who had yet to hear his voice. Moreover, far from recognizing any distinction between these 'other sheep' and the 'sheep', or any two-graded everlasting life, Jesus promises that 'there shall be one flock, one shepherd'.

That Jehovah's Witnesses can speak of the Body of Christ as 'limited to 144,000' is scarcely believable as we look elsewhere in the New Testament. Paul addresses *all* the Romans, *all* the Corinthians, *all* the Ephesians and *all* the

Colossians as members of Christ's Body. Similarly, the writer to the Hebrews appeals to *all* his readers to remember their fellow-Christians who are suffering on the grounds that they are all 'in the Body' (Romans 12:4–5; 1 Corinthians 10:17; Ephesians 1:23; Colossians 3:15; Hebrews 13:3). The teaching of the New Testament that every Christian is a member of Christ's Body is so clear that one can only conclude Jehovah's Witnesses do not see it because they do not wish to see it.

The future

As we saw earlier, Jehovah's Witnesses do not expect a visible return of the exalted Christ, but claim that the second coming took place in 1918. They now await the end of the present world-system which, they believe, will begin with the battle of Armageddon, when, so they assert, all the religious and political systems of the world will be ranged against Jehovah and his faithful Witnesses. Every earthquake, famine and large-scale catastrophe is seen as a sign that the end is imminent, and these are powerful incentives to the Witnesses in their proselytizing activities, for they firmly believe that only those who align themselves with Jehovah by becoming members of their sect will survive Armageddon. Everyone else will be annihilated.

After Armageddon, the devil will be locked up and there will be a thousand years of peace and life under what they describe as 'favourable conditions'. During the millennium, Jehovah's Witnesses will be actively reproducing to repopulate the world. Everyone will live throughout the period, but at the end of a thousand years the devil will be released for a short time to test those who have been born during it and have therefore never been really tested as to their loyalty to Jehovah. Those who survive this second probationary period will go on to live for ever, 144, 000 of them in heaven but the vast majority here on earth.

It will be seen, therefore, that (as was stated earlier) everlasting life according to the Watch Tower gospel is not a gift of God held out to those who put their trust in Christ, as the New Testament states, but is a reward earned through personal merit. Ephesians 2 makes clear how far removed from true Christianity such a belief is.

How they work

Having denied almost every cardinal doctrine of the Christian faith, Jehovah's Witnesses can in no sense of the word be regarded as Christians. Moreover, they are firmly convinced that they alone have the truth and that everyone else is wrong: only they have Jehovah's message for the world's salvation. In contrast, they believe, the Christian denominations are of the devil and their ministers are servants of Satan. This is the background against which we must try to understand their missionary outreach.

Most readers will be familiar with the first step in their strategy, the initial contact, for almost everyone living in Britain has been approached by a Jehovah's Witness at some time. The Witness knocks at your door (or confronts you on the street corner), introduces himself as one who would like to talk to you about God, or the Bible, or some recent disaster or current problem. At first he may hide the fact that he is a Jehovah's Witness. Much of what he says at this stage may appear to be harmless, for his chief aim is to win a hearing and then to leave a piece of his movement's literature with you.

If you show interest in his message and agree to accept a piece of literature, be it a copy of *The Watchtower* or *Awake* or a more substantial book such as *Good News to Make You Happy* or *The Truth that Leads to Everlasting Life,* you will be named in his records as an interested person worthy of another visit. This point needs to be underlined, for many people make the mistake of thinking that if they buy a magazine or book the Jehovah's Witness will go away and leave them alone. The surest way of guaranteeing further visits is to accept literature, for you are then named in the records submitted to headquarters and marked down for a back call.

During his second visit the Witness will be concerned, not merely to discuss religion with you and to ascertain your views about the literature left during the first visit, but also to persuade you to open your house for a home study group. He will explain that this is to be an informal Bible study and you will be asked to encourage members of your family and friends to attend it. 'Let's forget about the churches and simply study together what God has to say in his Word' will be typical of the approach at this stage. In reality, these sessions are always studies of one of the movement's latest books and are more like indoctrination sessions. Although the Bible is used, texts are taken out of their context in an attempt to show their support for Watch Tower doctrines. There will be no scope for differences of interpretation, for the 'true' view, and therefore the only acceptable one, will be the official line laid down in the Watch Tower book being studied.

If your interest persists, the next step will be to persuade you to join a larger group meeting in your area, consisting of some 'enquirers' like yourself and some convinced and committed Jehovah's Witnesses like your visitor. Here the pattern will be largely the same, the 'Bible' study being a study of one of the sect's books. The overriding aim all through will be to condition you to think as Jehovah's Witnesses think. Then you will be ready for the next step.

Jehovah's Witnesses do not usually make the mistake of inviting 'outsiders' to their Kingdom Hall meetings straight away, but wait until such people have been prepared by weeks of the kind of 'pre-evangelism' already outlined. But once there they are given a warm welcome and every effort is made to integrate them. Those whose interest now persists begin attending regularly. Every Sunday they will meet to study the latest edition of *The Watchtower*. Several weekday evenings they will be expected to attend lectures in the movement's doctrine and training sessions to equip them to communicate these doctrines on door steps and street corners and in home meetings. The movement is very thorough in its teaching-practice methods.

It is as people begin to undertake this work of witnessing that they are recognized by the sect as Jehovah's Witnesses. The next step is baptism by immersion, by which they dedicate themselves as servants of Jehovah.

This, then, is the typical strategy all Jehovah's Witnesses use in their efforts to win converts. The tactics may vary slightly from place to place and from individual to individual, but not much, for Jehovah's Witnesses are expected to keep to a fairly stereotyped and well-tried pattern in their proselytizing.

How to deal with them

It is difficult to write generally on this subject. Much will depend on the kind of person you are and the extent to which you have a grasp of basic Christian teaching. But here are one or two points which may help.

When the Jehovah's Witness confronts you on his initial visit, his intention will be to preach a short sermon gleaned from the current issue of *The Watchtower*. It may be useless to try to argue with him about this. He has received very careful instruction in every aspect of this subject and, if he has done his homework, will serve up all *The Watchtower* answers. But if you can divert him from this subject, or if you seize your opportunity when he pauses for breath, you may find that he is not nearly so sure of himself on other ground.

He will quote the Bible freely, but do not allow yourself to be drawn into an argument in which texts (usually out of their context) are thrown about between you. Get your Bible, look up the verse he mentions and insist on seeing it in its context. Refuse to move on to other texts until you have done this. You will find that often a Witness uses a text without understanding its meaning at all. Do not fall into the trap of allowing yourself to be linked with any kind of Jehovah's Witness study group, for, as stated earlier, the intention of such groups is to indoctrinate members in Jehovah's Witness teaching, not to study the Bible.

More important than anything else, talk to him about your personal faith in Christ. Show him that your religion is not the satanic thing he has been led to believe it to be, but a living, vital relationship with Christ. This is an experience to which his own movement can never lead him, for it has denied both Christ and the Holy Spirit. Give your personal testimony and pray that God will use it.

Anyone who seriously encounters Jehovah's Witnesses will naturally read two or three of their books in order to see their own presentation of what they believe. A fresh one is produced fairly frequently and the old ones are discarded. In order to get the feel of what it is like to be a member, one should read Ted Dencher's or Valerie Tomsett's book.

Summary of the main doctrinal differences

JEHOVAH'S WITNESSES   CHRISTIANS

Authority

Though claiming to accept the Bible as God's Word, members must accept it only as it is interpreted by the Watch Tower Society. Thus the Society, not the Bible, becomes the real authority.

The Bible is the yardstick against which all claims to truth are to be measured, including those made by earthly leaders claiming special gifts of interpretation.

God

God is one person, Jehovah. All other beings have been created by him, including his Son, Jesus Christ.

God is Father, Son and Holy Spirit, three Persons within the unity of the Godhead, who are coequal and coeternal.

Christ

Christ is a secondary god, inferior to the one true God, Jehovah. Though he pre-existed, he is not eternal. His incarnation is rejected.

Though he has always existed with his Father as the eternal Son of God, at his human birth he became man. As God and man he is the unique Saviour.

Spirit

The holy spirit is God's active but impersonal force at work in the world.

The Holy Spirit is the third Person of the Trinity, who not only works throughout God's universe but dwells within and empowers every Christian believer.

Salvation

Christ's death does not guarantee eternal life for anyone, but as a ransom for Adam's sin gives those who believe in Christ a second chance to earn eternal life under favourable conditions after they have been raised from the dead.

Achieved by Christ, who died and rose again for use, salvation is not something we earn but God's gracious gift which is to be appropriated through faith.

Church

Jehovah's Witnesses alone are Jehovah's faithful servants and therefore the only real Christians. Everyone else, including members of the churches of Christendom, are of the devil.	The one church consists of all those who through faith have accepted Jesus as Saviour and acknowledge him as Lord.

Future

Christ's second coming occurred invisibly in 1918. The Battle of Armageddon at the end of the world are imminent. Those who survive and then show their loyalty to Jehovah during the millennium will be rewarded with everlasting life, for 144,000 in heaven but for the majority on earth.	Though it is a sure and certain hope, promised in the Bible, no-one knows when the second coming will occur. All those whose trust is in Christ already possess eternal life, which they will one day enjoy in all its fullness in God's presence.

Notes

[1] *Let God Be True* (The Watch Tower Bible and Tract Society, revised edition 1952), p. 9.

[2] *Things in Which it is Impossible for God to Lie* (The Watch Tower Bible and Tract Society, 1965), p. 31.

[3] *The New World Translation* (The Watch Tower Bible and Tract Society).

[4] See the Appendix, p. 126.

[5] R. V. G. Tasker, *The Gospel according to St John.* Tyndale New Testament Commentary (Inter-Varsity Press, 1960), p. 45.

[6] *Things in Which it is Impossible for God to Lie,* p. 231.

[7] J. F. Rutherford, *The Harp of God* (The Watch Tower Bible and Tract Society, 1928), p. 103.

[8] *Make Sure of All Things* (The Watch Tower Bible and Tract Society, 1953), p. 360.

[9] *Things in Which it is Impossible for God to Lie,* p. 269.

For further reading

Alan Rogerson, *Millions Now Living Will Never Die: A Study of Jehovah's Witnesses* (Constable, 1969).

W. C. Stevenson, *Year of Doom, 1975* (Hutchinson, 1967).

Ted Dencher, *Why I left Jehovah's Witnesses* (Lakeland, 1973).

Valerie Tomsett, *Released from the Watchtower* (Lakeland, 1971).

3 Mormons

Unlike Jehovah's Witnesses, Mormons (otherwise known as members of the Church of Jesus Christ of Latter-day Saints) do not claim to recognize the final authority of the Bible in doctrinal matters. Instead, they believe that God still reveals his will through prophets and for them the chief of these prophets is the American founder of their movement, Joseph Smith.

Mormons believe that Smith's writings, *The Book of Mormon*, *Doctrine and Covenants* and *Pearl of Great Price*, are inspired utterances containing God's truth for his people in these 'latter-days'. Whereas they claim to accept the Bible as the Word of God in so far as it is translated correctly, they make no such qualification regarding the chief volume of their own scriptures. One of their leaders claimed that the manner in which *The Book of Mormon* was translated ruled out the possibility of any error, which is a strange claim when it is remembered that some 3,000 changes have been made in the text since the book's first appearance in 1830.[1] We shall see that, although Mormons pay lip-service to the Bible, their teaching stems very largely from these other books. That is why Le Grand Richards, one of the most important modern exponents of Mormonism, claimed that Mormonism was the only Christian church that did not depend entirely upon the Bible for its teaching. He added, 'If we had no Bible we would still have all the needed direction and information through the revelation of the Lord "to his servants the prophets" in these latter-days.'[2] The implication is clear. The additional Mormon scriptures are absolute necessities

41

for the modern Christian, but the Bible (though important) is an optional extra.

To evaluate this claim, it will be necessary to look in some detail at the story Mormons tell of how these divine revelations were mediated to modern man through their founder, Joseph Smith. We shall then examine the main Mormon beliefs, seeing how they differ from those of mainstream Christianity, before concluding with a brief outline of the methods Mormons use to spread their teaching.

A brief history

Joseph Smith (1805–44) came from a family popularly regarded as illiterate, drunken, irreligious and superstitious. He tells his own story in *Pearl of Great Price* and more briefly in the standard introduction to *The Book of Mormon*. As an adolescent he found himself bewildered by the many denominations and sects claiming people's allegiance. Attracted towards Methodism through a religious revival, inspired by a preacher named Lane, then affecting New York State where the Smith family lived, he was wondering whether to join this church when, so he claimed, he received his first vision. In 1820, in response to his prayer for guidance, Smith claimed that God the Father and his Son, Jesus Christ, appeared to him in a pillar of light, told him to join none of the existing denominations because their creeds were an abomination in God's sight, and indicated that Joseph was the divinely selected agent through whom real Christianity and the true church would be restored to the earth. Through this and subsequent visions he came to believe that he was destined to be God's mouthpiece, a nineteenth-century prophet chosen to recall Christendom from apostasy.

In a second vision which Smith claimed to receive three years later an angelic messenger named Moroni told him of the whereabouts of certain gold plates, containing the history of the former inhabitants of the American continent as well as a fullness of the gospel message hitherto unrevealed. These plates were said to be buried in a stone box on the side of a hill called Cumorah near Palmyra. Though Smith would find that the writing on the plates was in the form of ancient hieroglyphics, he would be able to translate them with the aid of a pair of supernaturally provided 'spectacles', two transparent stones set in a silver frame. As well as being told about the plates, Smith claims that he was also promised a special revelation about the priesthood. Accordingly, Smith said, he went to the designated spot on 22 September 1823 and found the box containing the plates. They were eight inches square and bound together by three large rings. The supernatural 'spectacles' were by their side. When he reached out to take hold of them, however, some supernatural power immobilized his arm. When in frustration he cried out, 'Why cannot I obtain this book?', Moroni informed him that his failure was because of pride. If Smith repented and remained faithful to God, he would be allowed to take possession of the plates at a later date. Exactly four years later, Smith maintained, he returned to the spot, was allowed to remove the plates and the 'spectacles', and began translating the hieroglyphics. Martin Harris, a farming friend, gave him some money and acted as his scribe.

Mormons have always claimed that Harris copied some of the characters from the plates and took these and Smith's translation of them to Professor Charles Anthon in New York. The professor is said to have confirmed both the authenticity of the characters and the accuracy of the translation. As we shall see, Anthon, who was Professor of Latin and Greek at Columbia University, told a different story.

Smith had to face an early setback when Lucy Harris, the sceptical wife of his scribe, stole the translation of the first 116 pages. She then taunted the Mormon founder by saying, 'If this be a divine communication, the same being who revealed it to you can easily replace it.' Smith's faith was apparently insufficient to rise to the challenge, however, for he answered lamely that God had forbidden him to retranslate those pages.

The translation was completed in 1829 and published on 18 March 1830 as *The Book of Mormon*. Smith explained that the gold plates were then handed back to Moroni who returned them to heaven. Martin Harris financed the first edition. It takes its name from a general named Mormon, who is said to have lived on the American continent about

AD 400, to have kept, abridged and supplemented the records of his ancestors, and to have handed them over to his son, Moroni, for safe keeping. Moroni in turn brought the records up to date and then buried the plates in the ground. Mormons believe that these were the plates unearthed by Smith in 1827 and that Moroni, by that time a resurrected being, was the divinely sent messenger who informed the Mormon founder of their location.

The book itself claims to give an account of the descendants of a prophet named Lehi, who left Jerusalem with his family 600 years before Christ and reached America, where he became the founding father of a mighty civilization. The Indians whom Columbus found when he discovered America are said to be 'the benighted remnants of a once mighty civilization'.[3] The book also contains an account of a visit Jesus Christ is said to have made to America following his death and resurrection in Palestine. Christ is seen repeating much of the teaching previously given to the original apostles and other disciples. The historical span of *The Book of Mormon* is said to cover the years 600 BC to AD 400.

Smith claimed eleven witnesses to the existence of the gold plates and their translation, and their sworn statements still appear in every copy of *The Book of Mormon*. Opinions obviously differ about the reliability of the testimony. Several of them afterwards left the Mormon Church. There can be little doubt, however, that in the movement's early days their witness contributed in no small way to its growth.

In the course of his visions in 1823, Smith claimed that he had also been informed that the true priesthood, forfeited centuries earlier by an apostate church, was about to be restored to the earth through him. He asserted that this promise was then fulfilled when John the Baptist descended from heaven in a cloud of light and ordained him and an early convert, Oliver Cowdery, to the Aaronic priesthood, promising that in due course they would also receive the Melchizedek priesthood. This promise was likewise fulfilled when the apostles Peter, James and John came to ordain them, appointed them as first and second elders of the Church, and gave Smith authority to organize the Church and the Kingdom of God upon earth. Accordingly, on 6 April

1830, soon after the publication of *The Book of Mormon*, Smith and five supporters founded the Church of Jesus Christ of Latter-day Saints at Fayette, New York State. A further revelation instructed church members to receive Smith's teaching as authoritative, God allegedly saying of the Mormon founder, 'His word ye shall receive, as if from mine own mouth.'[4] Before long, therefore, plans were being made to preserve Smith's utterances in print and there came into existence Smith's *Book of Commandments*, later to be renamed *Doctrine and Covenants*, and *Pearl of Great Price*. As we have seen, Mormons regard these books as scripture, and as more important than the Christian Bible in that they contain additional divine revelations.

Although Smith soon had many followers, he was also subjected to much ridicule and persecution, so he and his followers left New York State for Kirtland, Ohio. There he stayed for less than two years before further opposition led him to move first to Missouri and then to Illinois, where he and his followers built the city of Nauvoo. It was in Illinois that Smith's fourteen years as the Mormon leader came to a violent end. Smith and a number of church members were practising polygamy, and some of his closest friends, disillusioned, broke away from the Mormon Church and began to expose his immorality in a paper called the *Nauvoo Expositor*. Smith ordered their printing-office to be destroyed and, when they appealed to the state governor, Smith, his brother and two other Mormon leaders were arrested and remanded in custody to await trial. The trial never took place. A madly excited mob stormed the prison, the guards made only a half-hearted attempt to repel them, and Smith was murdered. The Mormon Church had been given its martyr.

Brigham Young then became leader of the main body of Mormons, guiding them on their historic trek across America to Utah, where they built Salt Lake City and founded what was to become the State of Utah. Despite much opposition from the United States federal government, polygamy continued until 1890. In that year, however, the Mormons yielded to government pressure and the threat of confiscation of property, and outlawed the practice. When Brigham Young died in 1877, he left behind him a strongly bureaucratic structure which has provided the Mormon Church's framework ever since. Today, Mormonism is a highly-organized and efficient movement, noted for its good works and with a strong emphasis on family life. Its leader, the First President, is still believed to be the mouthpiece of God, the agent through whom come divine revelations, though in practice such revelations are not accepted as God's word until they have received the approval of the Mormon Church's general conference.

There are two grades of priesthood. Aaronic priests are male Mormons between the ages of twelve and nineteen. Melchizedek priests are those of nineteen and over. Until 1978 Negroes, like women, were barred from the priesthood, but on 9 June of that year the President announced that 'all worthy male members of the Church may be ordained to the priesthood without regard for race or colour'. This change of policy was justified on the grounds that it had been indicated in another God-given revelation to the Mormon Church through its President. The truth appears to be that once more (as previously over the question of polygamy) Mormon leaders have yielded to the mounting pressure of public opinion. Perhaps in time women will also be eligible for ordination to the priesthood.

Whether male or female, ordained or not, every Mormon is regarded as a missionary, is expected to tithe his income, must abstain from tea, coffee, alcohol and tobacco, and is encouraged (if young enough) to undertake a missionary tour in another country. There are about three million Mormons in the world, about half of them in the American State of Utah. A British temple was dedicated near Lingfield, Surrey in 1958 and, like all other Mormon temples, provides secret rites for members, including the practices of vicarious baptism and celestial marriage. Mormon missionaries have been active in Britain almost from the beginning of the Mormon Church and in the middle of the nineteenth century many thousands of converts left Britain to settle in Utah. The present membership of the Mormon Church in Britain is about 80,000.

Is it a fairy story?

Mormons and non-Mormons can at least agree on one thing: Mormonism stands or falls on the genuineness of the Mormon claims about the origin of *The Book of Mormon*. Was Joseph Smith telling the truth about his visions, the plates and the translation? Or was he a fraud who made up the story for what he could get out of it? Or was he, perhaps, a sadly deluded man who was more to be pitied than blamed? We must consider the evidence.

Where are the plates today?

Were they in existence, they could be submitted to various tests and to the eye of honest research. Then it would soon be shown whether they were as old as Mormons claim. The Mormon answer is far from convincing, for they claim that Smith was ordered to return the plates to the safe keeping of the angel Moroni when the work of translation was completed. That seems too easy a way out of a very awkward situation!

Does Smith's character inspire confidence?

Though Jesus Christ made some tremendous claims, those claims were authenticated by the life he lived and, most of all, by the vindication of his resurrection. Joseph Smith, in contrast, does not appear to have been the kind of man that everyone could trust. He was regarded as a rogue by some of those who knew him best. Four years before the publication of *The Book of Mormon* and the founding of the Mormon Church, he was found guilty of being 'a disorderly person and an impostor'.[5] Fawn Brodie, one of his fairest biographers, says that his reputation before he organized his church was that of 'a likable ne'er-do-well' who was 'notorious for tall stories and necromantic arts' and who spent his leisure leading a band of idlers in digging for buried treasure.[6]

We also have to bear in mind Smith's polygamy. He himself claimed divine authority for this practice, though, as we have seen, the practice was outlawed in the Mormon Church from 1890 onwards. Is a man who commanded his followers to take several wives, and who himself set them the

47

example, the kind of person to inspire confidence as God's mouthpiece to modern civilization?

What about the expert testimony?

As we have seen, Smith claimed that Professor Charles Anthon of Columbia University vouched for the genuineness of the characters Smith copied from the gold plates and for the accuracy of the Mormon founder's translation. Unfortunately for the Mormons, Anthon's story is rather different. In a letter written to E. D. Howe in 1834, the professor stated quite categorically, 'The whole story about my having pronounced the Mormonite inscription to be "reformed Egyptian hieroglyphics" is perfectly false.'[7] He agreed that a man did bring him a piece of paper containing what he described as a 'singular scrawl' and which he believed had been copied from a book containing various alphabets. At first, Anthon thought it was a hoax and treated it rather light-heartedly, but when the man told him about the gold plates and mentioned that he had been asked for money to publish the translation, he concluded that it was 'a scheme to cheat the farmer of his money'.

It is worth remembering that Anthon's letter was written only four years after the publication of *The Book of Mormon*. Mormons claim that in this letter Anthon was lying and that originally he had indeed vouched for the inscription's genuineness but later changed his mind. It is hard to find a motive for such action. Would a reputable professor risk his reputation because of blind prejudice against the Mormons? Today, therefore, we are faced with this paradoxical situation. On the one hand, Mormons claim that Anthon was a reliable witness to the authenticity of the copied characters, but on the other hand that he was a liar when he wrote his letter to Howe. If the Mormon version of the incident is true, then it raises questions about Anthon's reliability to vouch for the inscription in the first place. If Anton's version is true, then the Mormons have no independent evidence to substantiate their claim about the characters and Smith's alleged translation.

Can we trust the 'three' and the 'eight'?

As stated earlier, every copy of *The Book of Mormon* contains sworn statements from eleven witnesses to its authenticity. The first three were among Smith's chief supporters in the early days of Mormonism. Like him, they were anxious that the movement should succeed and they would be prepared to back up his story. All three later left the Mormon Church and were branded by their former colleagues as rogues and counterfeiters. Were they any more trustworthy when they were still Mormons? Even if we take their evidence at its face value, however, it amounts to no more than that they had a vision in the neighbouring woods when the angel laid the plates before their eyes, not that they saw the plates as Smith was translating them. As for the other eight witnesses, it is worth noting their names. Four were Whitmers and three were Smiths; the eighth married a Whitmer daughter. As one Roman Catholic writer has said, 'It is altogether too close a family circle.'[8]

What archaeological evidence is there for the claims of The Book of Mormon?

Smith claimed that the gold plates contained the history of the ancient inhabitants of America, as well as the fullness of the everlasting gospel. This involves the belief that two great civilizations once existed on the American continent, that millions of people populated that part of the world, and that all of this began with the exodus of a small group of people from Israel many years before Christ. According to one writer, however, 'leading archaeological researchers have not only repudiated the claims of *The Book of Mormon* as to the existence of these civilizations, but have adduced considerable evidence to show the impossibility of the accounts given in the Mormon Bible'. This writer quotes the words of W. Duncan Strong of New York's Columbia University: 'I do not believe that there is a single thing of value concerning the pre-history of the American Indian in *The Book of Mormon* and I believe the great majority of American archaeologists would agree with me.'[9]

How do Mormons account for the large sections of the Authorized Version of the Bible which are found in The Book of Mormon?

The book is supposed to cover the period from 600 BC to AD 400. Whoever compiled it, however, appears to have had a copy of the Authorized Version of the Bible before him, and that translation dates from AD 1611. This seems to be the only satisfactory explanation of the facts. Comparisons of Isaiah 2 – 14 and 2 Nephi 12 – 24, Isaiah 48 – 49 and 2 Nephi 20 – 21, and Malachi 3 – 4 and 3 Nephi 24 – 25 are most revealing in this respect. Many more instances of this 'borrowing' occur throughout *The Book of Mormon.*

Mormons try to avoid the charge of plagiarism by maintaining that, because Smith knew the language of the Authorized Version so well, it was inevitable that he would use the language of that version in translating *The Book of Mormon.* It has to be remembered, however, that what we are confronted with in *The Book of Mormon* are not occasional AV-sounding phrases and verses but rather whole blocks, sometimes many chapters, of actual AV material, along with some of the established inaccuracies of that particular translation of the Bible. However Mormons try to avoid the conclusion, therefore, the facts speak for themselves. Whoever wrote *The Book of Mormon* had the Authorized Version of the Bible (or a book containing many quotations from it) before him and copied large sections from it. This completely demolishes the Mormon claim that the book in its original form was completed around AD 400.

Are the claims of The Book of Mormon reasonable?

Is it reasonable to accept, for example, the authenticity of a book which maintains that a detailed Christian theology was being proclaimed as early as the sixth century before Christ? It is true that Mormons say the writer is setting out this theology prophetically to prepare for Christ's first coming. A more reasonable explanation is that *The Book of Mormon* is a product of the nineteenth century. Mormons, however, expect us to believe that, whereas the Old Testament writers foresaw the coming of Christ in dark shadows, as early as 600 BC their own prophet Nephi was given detailed visions in which most of the events of Christ's life shone as brightly as the noonday sun. Readers of 1 Nephi 11:13ff. and 2 Nephi 2:6ff. will find recorded details about the virgin birth, the divine sonship of Christ, the baptism of Jesus by John the Baptist, Christ's ministry of teaching, healing and casting out devils, his fellowship with the twelve apostles, his atoning death on the cross, and his triumphant resurrection. Good though it is to read about such things in *The Book of Mormon*, it does not seem likely that they could ever have been written down six centuries before they actually happened – and in the AV language of 1611!

The Mormon 'myth'

Trying to be kind to the Mormons and attempting to help them out of their obvious difficulties about *The Book of Mormon*, some well-meaning mainstream Christians have suggested that we do Mormonism a disservice by taking their claims literally and then raising intellectual arguments against such claims. What we should do, they maintain, is to regard the story of angelic visitations, gold plates and supernatural spectacles as part of the great Mormon myth. The implication is that what matters is not whether the story itself is true, but rather whether it is a good literary vehicle for an essentially religious message. It needs to be stated quite categorically, however, that far from finding this attitude helpful, Mormons themselves will have no truck with it. To them the whole story is literally true and has to be swallowed, hook, line and sinker. So in evaluating the Mormon claim we are back where we began. The Mormon religion stands or falls on the genuineness of the Mormon claim about the origin, discovery and translation of *The Book of Mormon*. It is my firm belief that anyone who firmly resolves to examine the hard evidence, and who does not allow himself to be sidetracked by Mormon religious subjectivism, will be compelled to conclude that, whatever else *The Book of Mormon* may or may not be, it is certainly not what Mormons from 1830 to the present day claim it to be, an additional and essential volume of scripture with further divine revelations for God's people living in these latter-days.

The other Mormon scriptures

As mentioned earlier, Mormons regard two other volumes, *Doctrine and Covenants* and *Pearl of Great Price*, as inspired scripture, containing God's word to his people living in these latter-days. Sections 1 to 133 of *Doctrine and Covenants* claim to be revelations given by God to or through Joseph Smith; section 134 is 'A Declaration of Belief regarding Governments and Laws'; section 135 tells the story of Smith's 'martyrdom'; section 136 contains 'The Word and Will of the Lord, given through President Brigham Young', Smith's successor. Smith's 133 revelations were received between September 1823 and July 1843. It seems that whenever Smith wished his followers to accept some new doctrine or rules regarding the organization of his growing movement, he received a timely revelation giving his words divine authority.

These revelations include the well-known abstinence rule (section 89) instructing Mormons to abstain from tobacco, wine, strong drink and hot drinks (*i.e.* tea and coffee), and to eat meat only in moderation, all of which are still required of every Mormon.

The most far-reaching and controversial revelation was section 132, by which Smith sought to justify his unorthodox views concerning marriage. He claimed two things. First, he said that whereas ordinary marriage was a covenant that came to an end when one of the partners died, if the partners made a marriage covenant for eternity their marriage would survive the separation of death and they would be re-united as man and wife after the resurrection. On the basis of this view, Mormons have a ceremony called Celestial Marriage, which has to be performed in one of their temples and which, they claim, is absolutely essential, not only for ensuring their marriages survive physical death, but also to ensure that they attain to the highest grade of salvation.

Smith's second claim in section 132 was much more sensational, for he maintained that God had given him the right to practise polygamy and to enjoin his followers to do the same. There is evidence that Smith and some of his followers had begun to practise polygamy long before this 'revelation' and that the revelation was proclaimed to justify their actions.

Smith's bitterest opponents have always maintained, therefore, that the revelation was intended to give respectability to the prophet's illicit love affairs.

As we have seen, Mormons gave up this practice in 1890, as they are very careful to point out in their missionary work. The polygamy question is still important, however, because of its bearing upon the Mormon view of scripture. Mormons still regard *Doctrine and Covenants* as the word of God and section 132 is certainly still to be found in modern editions of that volume. When it came to the choice of either complying with this revelation and having their property confiscated, on the one hand, or obeying the federal government and being granted statehood, on the other, Mormons chose to go back on Smith and obey the civil authority.

Because of their fundamentalist attitude to their own scriptures, Mormons have always found section 132 something of an embarrassment. If they were able to admit that in this particular instance Smith had been wrong, they could discard section 132 from *Doctrine and Covenants*. For them, however, it remains as part of inspired scripture, but paradoxically as a part of scripture which must not be obeyed on pain of excommunication. Some Mormons, perhaps unconsciously admitting the inconsistency of this position, look forward to the days of the millennium when the need for such expediency will disappear and they will be able to reintroduce the practice and thus obey God's command. Others argue that it was an interim arrangement, designed specifically for a time when Mormons were a very small minority and needed such a practice to increase the number of Mormon children. Whatever rationalization occurs, however, the inconsistency of the Mormon position remains. If Smith was right in proclaiming section 132 as a God-given revelation, then polygamy should have continued no matter what the cost. Of course, if Smith was wrong, no problem exists for non-Mormons. For obvious reasons, however, Mormons cannot admit that their founder was in error, for if it could be shown that he was mistaken about this 'revelation', who could say when he was right in the others? And if he were proved unreliable in *Doctrine and Covenants*, to what extent could *The Book of Mormon* and *Pearl of Great Price* be trusted?

Pearl of Great Price completes the Mormon scriptures. Despite its name, it has little of real value to offer. It contains the Authorized Version of Matthew 24 with a few minor variations and Smith's version of some of the early chapters of Genesis. There is also an alleged translation from a papyrus which was said to have been discovered in the Egyptian catacombs and which, so Smith claimed, contains the writings of Abraham when he was in Egypt. Until recently it was believed that the manuscript evidence for this part of *Pearl of Great Price* was destroyed in a Chicago museum fire in 1970. According to anti-Mormon sources, however, that papyrus has now come to light. Far from vindicating Smith, it proves he knew no Egyptian and shows that what he regarded as the writings of Abraham are parts of funeral texts from the Egyptian *Book of Breathings*.

For obvious reasons, we have spent a long time considering the validity of the Mormon scriptures. If Smith's claim to be a true prophet with an inspired message from God turns out to be completely false, then there is little point in concerning ourselves unduly with the other doctrines of the church he founded. After examining the evidence against the Mormon claims for *The Book of Mormon*, and after taking a brief look at *Doctrine and Covenants* and *Pearl of Great Price*, we may fairly conclude that, whatever else these books may be, they are certainly not the inspired Word of God. As we go on now to consider briefly some of the other doctrines of Mormonism, it will be seen that they are a distortion of the true Word of God contained in the Christian Bible.

Some Mormon doctrines

God

At the outset of this brief discussion of Mormon beliefs, it must be remembered that, although Mormon writers often use orthodox terminology, the views behind this terminology are far from orthodox. This is particularly true of their view of God. Although they are ready to speak of a threefold God and, on occasions, even of a trinity, they are totally opposed to the Christian view of the Trinity (see Appendix).

Mormons believe that God is tangible. Arguing from the

Genesis statement that man is made in God's image, they maintain that God is like us and must have a physical body of flesh and bones every bit as real as our bodies. They believe that Deuteronomy 4:28 supports this view. Le Grand Richards, for example, maintains that the true God, as contrasted with the idols mentioned in Deuteronomy, can see, hear, eat and smell, and must, therefore, possess a physical body with the organs enabling him to do these things.[10] Looking at the verse in its context, however, we can see it demands a very different interpretation, for the whole purpose of this section of Deuteronomy is to forbid the making of idols on the grounds that, when God spoke to Israel, they heard his voice but saw no form. Significantly, Richards does not quote verses 15–18 of the same chapter; 'On the day when the Lord spoke to you out of the fire on Horeb, you saw no figure of any kind; so take good care not to fall into the degrading practice of making figures carved in relief, in the form of a man or a woman, or of an animal on earth or bird that flies in the air, or of any reptile on the ground or fish in the waters under the earth' (NEB). In its context, ignored by Richards and other Mormon writers, Deuteronomy argues strongly against God's tangibility.

The idea of an evolving God is also an integral part of Mormon theology. They believe that the Supreme God is, as it were, at the top of the ladder, whilst we are beginning to ascend near the bottom. Even God has not always been at the top, they claim, but has climbed up from those rungs on which we now stand. In his funeral address for Elder King Follett (1844) Smith said, 'God himself was once as we are now, and is an exalted man.' Lorenzo Smith made a similar statement which has become a maxim of Mormon doctrine: 'As man is, God once was; as God is, man may become.' Mormon writings abound with this kind of teaching.

Logically, Mormons also believe in a plurality of gods, for there is, they maintain, a Council of the Gods over whom the Supreme God presides. As well as Jesus Christ, this Council includes Enoch, Elijah, Abraham, Peter, Paul, and many more recent characters including Joseph Smith and Brigham Young. In the funeral address already quoted Joseph Smith told his hearers, 'You have got to learn how to be Gods yourselves...the same as all Gods have done before you, namely by going from one small degree to another.' Such teaching leads W. R. Martin to conclude that Mormonism is 'polytheistic to the core'.[11]

Bible readers will not need to be told how unscriptural such views are. They are completely repudiated by such passages as Exodus 20:1–6, and Isaiah 40:12–31 and 45:18, which (along with many others) stress that the Lord God is one, sovereign and eternal God, besides whom there is no other God.

Jesus Christ

The Mormon view of Christ has to be seen against the background of their doctrine of God, where Jesus Christ figures among the other 'gods' of the Council of the Gods. It also has to be interpreted in the light of the Mormon doctrine of the pre-existence of all spirits, for Mormonism holds that our pre-existent spirits were all 'begotten by Heavenly Parents even as Jesus was'. The implications are very serious. Either Christ is a creature like us, or we are part of the Godhead like him. In both cases the essential uniqueness of Christ, as upheld in the Scriptures, disappears completely. He is no different from us. This means that some of the more orthodox Mormon descriptions of Christ as God, Jehovah and Eternal are emptied of much of their meaning.

The Holy Spirit

Mormons distinguish between the Holy Ghost, whom they are ready to call 'the third personage of the Godhead', and the Spirit of God or of Christ. They say the Holy Ghost works only in those who have been baptized as Mormons and have received the laying-on of hands of the Mormon priesthood. The Spirit of God (or the Spirit of Christ), on the other hand, is the one who enlightens every man coming into the world irrespective of faith. Mormons further describe the Holy Ghost as a personage who may manifest himself in the form of a man (1 Nephi 11:11). Although his power and influence may affect anyone, in his actual person, they say, he has a located existence and is therefore confined to a limited space.

There is no scriptural justification for distinguishing between the Holy Ghost and the Spirit of God or of Christ. It is true that in the Bible the Holy Spirit is given various titles such as the Spirit of God, the Spirit of the Lord and the Spirit of Christ, but different titles do not denote different spirits. On the contrary, just as Son of man, Son of God and only begotten Son are all used of the one Lord Jesus Christ, so also the various titles of the Spirit all refer to the third Person of the Godhead. Moreover, the New Testament makes it clear that this one Holy Spirit, because he is God, is present everywhere. In fact, it is his presence within a person that makes that person a Christian, and when he dwells within it may truly be said that the Father and the Son also dwell within (Romans 8:9).

Salvation

'Not one of our Father's children is born in spiritual darkness,' state the Mormons. 'Little children are alive in Christ even from the foundation of the world.'[12] They go on to assert that our very presence in this world is an indication that in our previous spiritual existence we proved ourselves worthy to be born. Life here on earth, therefore, is a second probationary period. Those who pass this test successfully will progress towards godhood; for, as we have seen, one of Mormonism's chief incentives is expressed in the maxim, 'As man is, God once was; as God is, man may become.'

Christians believe that despite their sin they have been redeemed and saved to the uttermost by virtue of the death and resurrection of Christ (Ephesians 2:1–8). They are confident that in Christ they have already passed from death to life and that they have begun to enjoy eternal life as a present possession (John 5:24). In contrast, Mormons believe there are different grades of salvation or exaltation (as they prefer to describe it), and that whereas 'some degree of salvation will come to all who have not forfeited their right to it, exaltation is given only to those who by righteous effort have won a claim to God's merciful liberality'.[13] What this means in reality is that the only people who can hope to reach the highest grade are those who have submitted themselves to every Mormon ordinance. Thus the Mormon way of exaltation becomes faith *plus* baptism by immersion for the remission of sins *plus* the laying-on of hands by a Mormon priest for the gift of the Holy Ghost *plus* celestial marriage in a Mormon temple – and so on!

In places Mormon writers seem to be expressing orthodox Christian views regarding the work of Christ for our salvation. Le Grand Richards, for example, says that Christ 'redeemed us from the fall; he paid the price; he offered himself as a ransom'. A little later, however, he completely repudiates the doctrine of justification by faith alone. As one reads his book carefully, one discovers that what Mormons believe is that Christ died to free us from the consequences of Adam's sin (*i.e.* physical death), leaving us free to work for our own salvation. Richards goes on to state, 'Christ atoned for Adam's sin, leaving us responsible for our own sins…We free ourselves from the consequences of a broken law, and entitle ourselves to the blessings predicated upon obedience to divine law…Hence, as we continue our quest to know and understand the laws of God, and obey them, we increase the measure of our salvation or exaltation.'[14]

Baptism has such an important place in this Mormon scheme of salvation that Mormons are expected to be baptized vicariously for their dead relatives so that they too may be given a chance to be saved. Their concern to promote baptism for the dead accounts for the great interest among Mormons in genealogical research; to this end clergy are constantly being asked by Mormons for permission to make microfilm copies of parish registers.

The Christian view of salvation is very different. Although man was created perfect, he corrupted himself through disobedience and became a fallen creature with a natural bias towards evil. Moreover, man becomes in practice what he is by birth, a sinner; and as a sinner he is subject to God's just wrath and condemnation. God, however, has provided the way out in his Son. Because of what Christ has done by offering himself on the cross as a ransom for our sin, we can be reconciled to God and can receive God's gift of eternal life. *We* cannot work for it; Christ has earned it for us and we receive it by putting our trust in him. But when we have received salvation through faith, we go on in the power of God's Spirit to live and work to his praise and glory. We are saved not *through* works but *for* works, as Ephesians 2:8ff. makes quite clear.

The future

Mormons believe there will be a twofold gathering process before Christ returns to the earth to reign for a thousand years: the gathering of the Latter-day Saints in an American Zion and the gathering of the Jews around the Palestinian Jerusalem. During the millennium, Mormons will engage in a threefold task, building temples, baptizing for the dead and preaching. The preaching will be aimed at those who, though not Mormons, have been considered worthy enough to remain on earth during this period. All who live on during this thousand years will reach the age of a hundred and will then be suddenly changed to immortality. The wicked, though dead physically, will survive spiritually, and will have another chance to repent and cleanse themselves through suffering. Then, when the millennium comes to an end, all will take part in the second resurrection and will be judged. A renewed earth will then become the abode of those found worthy of the highest grade of salvation, the remainder of the human race being housed elsewhere. The damned, that is a third of the spirit world who rebelled before the world was made and a fairly small number of human beings guilty of the worst sins and therefore beyond the possibility of repentance and salvation, will spend eternity in hell.

How Mormons work

The Mormon Church has a great army of more than 12,000 young missionaries who give two years of their life to work full-time wherever their church cares to send them. There can be few readers who have not come into contact with such missionaries, and perhaps been greatly impressed with their sincerity and sacrificial zeal. Mormon literature claims that such missionaries, who do their missionary work at their own expense, make more than 180,000 converts a year in the 51 countries in which they work.

In recent years the Mormon missionary movement in Great Britain has been directed chiefly towards the new housing areas. Here the key to their strategy has been the erection of magnificent chapels which have become the envy of all other religious groups. These buildings act, not only as chapels for informal and friendly services and as schools for the instruction of Mormon members, but also as recreational and cultural centres. They provide a wide range of activities and excellent facilities and attract potential converts.

These excellent buildings are also used as local head-quarters for missionary drives and from them Mormon missionaries proceed in pairs to their door-to-door work in their areas. In an average three-hour session a Mormon pair may knock on as many as eighty doors and contact fifty people. Probably no more than five will be prepared to discuss religion with the missionaries, but perhaps two of these five will wish to know more and will follow the sugges-tion that they should arrange home-meetings at which Mormon views may be discussed more carefully.

Two other more subtle approaches made recently are the home entertainments evenings and open-air displays. In the first, Mormon missionaries, often without identifying them-selves, will offer to provide an evening's entertainment for the family. It is only as the evening draws to its close that the audience is given any indication of the religious motive behind the activity. The open-air displays take place in strategic areas such as shopping precincts or entrances to underground stations. By means of large and artistically produced display-stands the attention of passers-by is focused upon a theme such as that of family life. Once again, the religious affiliation of the 'attendants' may be hidden at first, but once contact is made the Mormons begin their missionary work.

Whatever method is used in missionary work, the main purpose is to convince contacts that whereas the orthodox Christian churches have lost their direction and have forsaken God's way, the Church of Jesus Christ of Latter-day Saints offers a restored gospel given through Joseph Smith which will lead people into the truth. The ultimate aim is to convince people that only within the Mormon church will they find salvation.

How to deal with them

On the whole, Mormon missionaries are not nearly as well-drilled in the doctrines of their movement as are Jehovah's Witnesses in theirs. This is especially true of those Mormons who have just begun their two-year stint. They learn as they go along! Because of this, they are sometimes susceptible to a reasoned Christian approach from one who has taken the trouble to think through his Christian position.

We have tried to show that the fundamental difference between Mormons and Christians is that of authority, for Mormons insist that God's fuller revelation has been given to the world through Joseph Smith. As we have seen, there are grave deficiencies in the evidence they provide to support this view. Sometimes Mormon missionaries can be made to think, if the inadequacy of their evidence is pointed out to them. This assumes, of course, that the Christian has taken the trouble to examine the Mormon claims and read some Mormon and non-Mormon literature. *The Book of Mormon* may be borrowed from most public libraries along with Robert Mullen's pro-Mormon historical survey, *The Mormons*. Most libraries also carry that thorough and well-documented life of Smith, *No Man Knows My History,* by Fawn Brodie. *The Maze of Mormonism,* by W. R. Martin, is an excellent evangelical critique of the movement, and a recent assessment of Mormonism is Maurice Burrell's *Wide of the Truth.*

In any discussion with Mormons, it is best to concentrate on some of the key issues, such as their beliefs about God, Christ and salvation, rather than to get side-tracked on secondary issues such as baptism for the dead, grades of salvation and abstinence from tea, coffee and alcohol. Moreover, in such discussions the Christian is well advised to keep the discussion rooted in biblical material. Little is to be gained by excursions into the additional Mormon scriptures, and as in any case Mormons accept the Bible as God's Word, here is common ground. Try to point out that God would not contradict himself, so what he says about himself, his Son, and sin and salvation in the Bible must stand. If the extraneous 'revelations' of Mormonism disagree, so much the worse for them!

It needs to be remembered, however, that the Christian is not aiming to win an argument but to witness for Christ. As in approaches to Jehovah's Witnesses, therefore, personal testimony to Christ is all-important. Tell them what Christ means to you and pray that God will use your witness.

The Reorganised Latter-day Saints

Throughout this chapter we have dealt exclusively with the main body of Mormons, those who operate from Salt Lake City and with whom the reader is most likely to come into contact. There have been schisms within the movement, however, and the Reorganised Church of Jesus Christ of Latter-Day saints has a following in this country and elsewhere. In some important respects, the Reorganised Mormons differ from the main body.[15] In particular, the Reorganised Church claims that its members are the true successors of Joseph Smith, that Smith never practised polygamy, and that Brigham Young and today's Utah Mormons are apostates.

Summary of the main doctrinal differences

MORMONS   CHRISTIANS

Authority

The Bible, though God's Word, contains a partial and inadequate record of God's revelation. *The Book of Mormon, Doctrine and Covenants* and *Pearl of Great Price* complete what is lacking in the Bible and are also God's Word. God continues to reveal his will through the Mormon priesthood, and especially through the Mormon President, who is regarded as a prophet.

God has revealed all that he wants us to know of himself and his will for us in the Person and teaching of Christ, his incarnate Word. All that we know of Christ is contained in the Bible, the written Word. The Bible is the yardstick against which all claims to truth are to be measured, including those made by earthly leaders claiming a prophetic gift.

God

Though Mormons use trinitarian language, the orthodox Christian view of the Trinity is rejected. God is believed to have a physical male body, to have evolved to his divine status from manhood, and to be one of a plurality of similar divine beings.

God is Father, Son and Holy Spirit, three coequal and coeternal Persons within the unity of the Godhead. The difference between God and man is not merely one of degree, but one of nature. God is creator, we are his creatures.

Christ

Though acknowledged as God's Son, Mormons believe that he (like his Father) differs from human beings only in the degree to which he has progressed.

He is the eternal Son of the eternal Father. He became incarnate, taking up our humanity into his Godhood, for our salvation. In his unique Person, the divine and the human natures are united.

Salvation

Mormons reject the idea of original sin. All will be saved (or exalted), but the degree of a person's salvation is dependent upon his obedience and in particular upon his acceptance of the Mormon ordinances of baptism, laying-on of hands, *etc*.

Achieved by Christ, who died and rose again for us, salvation is not something we earn, but God's gracious gift to be appropriated by faith. Full salvation is offered to all who put their trust in Christ. We obey God, not because by doing so we hope to achieve salvation, but because we love him.

Church

The Mormon Church (The Church of Jesus Christ of Latter-day Saints) is believed to be the Restored Church and therefore the only true Church, and its priests are regarded as the only true priests of God.

The one true church, which is the church founded on the apostles and prophets with Christ as the corner stone, consists of all who have accepted Christ as Saviour and acknowledge him as Lord. The whole church is 'a holy priesthood', though within its membership some are called to specific roles of leadership.

Future

Zion will be established in America, the Jews will be gathered in Palestine, and Christ will return. During the ensuing millennium, Mormon missionary work will continue. The day of judgment will follow.

The whole of history will be consummated when Christ returns and the faithful will then enjoy God's presence eternally.

Notes

1. Professor Anthony Hoekema notes some of these changes in *The Four Major Cults* (Paternoster Press, 1969), p. 84.
2. Le Grand Richards, *A Marvelous Work and a Wonder* (Deseret Book Company, Salt Lake City, 1950), p. 1.
3. *The Book of Mormon and You,* a leaflet used in Mormon missionary work.
4. *Doctrine and Covenants* 21:5.
5. Fawn M. Brodie, *No Man Knows My History* (Knopf, 1971), p. 16.
6. *Ibid.*
7. Cited by W. R. Martin in *The Maze of Mormonism* (Zondervan, 1962), p. 42.
8. Dr Leslie Rumble, in *The Homiletic and Pastoral Review,* December 1959.
9. W. R. Martin, *op. cit.,* p. 46.
10. Le Grand Richards, *op. cit.,* p. 14.
11. W. R. Martin, *op. cit.,* p. 81.
12. Le Grand Richards, *op. cit.,* p. 100.
13. J. E. Talmage, *Articles of Faith* (Mormon Church, 1908), p. 91.
14. Le Grand Richards, *op. cit.,* pp. 279ff.
15. See Maurice Burrell, *Wide of the Truth* (Marshall, Morgan and Scott, 1972).

4 Christadelphians

Like most of the sects on the perimeter of Christendom, the Christadelphians originated in America during the nineteenth century. Unlike Jehovah's Witnesses, Mormons and Christian Scientists, however, this movement was founded by an Englishman, Dr John Thomas. Thomas, the son of a Congregational minister, was born in Hoxton Square, London, on 12 April 1805. After studying medicine at St Thomas's Hospital, London, and qualifying as an MRCS, he set sail for America in 1832, intending to practise medicine there. Having survived a shipwreck on the way, however, he felt he owed it to God to devote the rest of his life to religion. For a time he continued to practise medicine alongside his religious activities and was awarded an American MD in 1848. Eventually, however, he gave up medicine completely and worked full-time to propagate his religious views, founding the Christadelphians, a title which means 'brothers in Christ'.

Thomas had become a keen student of the Bible, especially of the more difficult sections of the prophets and the book of Revelation. He was so sure that his own interpretations were right that he was ready not merely to reject many of the tenets of orthodox Christianity, but also to maintain that only those who accepted his views and became Christadelphians could be saved. In 1834, when still only 29, he began to publish his views in a magazine called *The Apostolic Advocate* and this was followed in 1844 by *The Herald of the Future Age*. He returned to England in 1848 and stayed for two years, preaching all over the country and writing what was to become a great Christadelphian classic, *Elpis Israel— An Exposition of the Kingdom of God*.

This rather heavy-going book of 450 pages was not very well received at first, but when Thomas made a second brief visit to England in 1862 he found many small groups of Thomasites, as they were first known, meeting in various parts of the country. According to the sociologist, Dr Bryan Wilson,[1] there were now flourishing Christadelphian centres in Birmingham, Nottingham, Aberdeen, Halifax and Edinburgh. At first the movement had no official headquarters, the members simply meeting for breaking-of-bread ceremonies in each other's houses, but it was not long before Birmingham began to emerge as the most influential centre, and other Christadelphians began to look to it for guidance and for a supply of lecturers. It was during this second visit that Thomas wrote a 2,000-page commentary on the book of Revelation which he called *Eureka* and in which he claimed he had solved problems of interpretation that had baffled biblical scholars for years.

By 1865 Thomas's followers throughout the world numbered about 1,000, the majority of them being found in Great Britain. Growth was steady, if unspectacular, and three years later there were twenty-five Christadelphian assemblies (or ecclesias, as they were called) in England, four in Wales and twelve in Scotland.

One of Thomas's earliest converts was Robert Roberts, who soon secured his position as British leader of the movement by publishing a magazine called *The Ambassador of the Coming Age*. Thomas made his third and final visit to Britain in 1869 and suggested that the magazine should be renamed *The Christadelphian*. When Thomas died on 5 March 1871, just as he was contemplating returning to this country permanently, Roberts took over the complete leadership of the movement and began to disseminate official Christadelphian views through *The Christadelphian*, the method used to propagate orthodox Christadelphianism ever since. Birmingham is still the headquarters of the main body of Christadelphians, though some splinter groups look elsewhere for their doctrinal leads.[2]

Roberts, developing many of Thomas's embryonic ideas,

wrote a detailed treatment of his views in *Christendom Astray*, a book which was intended, as its title makes clear, to demonstrate the wide gulf between Christadelphian and orthodox Christian teachings. It has been reprinted many times as a standard textbook. Throughout the book, Roberts emphasized that whereas Christianity, as represented by the churches of the various denominations, had turned its back on the Bible, Christadelphianism had based its views entirely upon the Scriptures.

The Christadelphians are essentially a lay movement and there are no professional clergy or ministers. Local ecclesias are run by male members and a very high proportion of the movement's membership takes a full part in its activities. Regular meetings include a weekly breaking-of-bread ceremony, a Sunday evening lecture intended for the public at large, a weekly Bible class and a women's meeting. Evangelistic work of a rather sober kind is intellectual in tone and is carried out through public lectures, personal contacts, well-organized and well-publicized Bible exhibitions, and attractive literature.

There are probably about 25,000 Christadelphians in Great Britain and fewer than that number in the rest of the world. They are one of the smaller sects, therefore, as Mormons, Jehovah's Witnesses and Christian Science have memberships that run into millions. Christadelphians are sometimes confused with Jehovah's Witnesses and in some respects their teachings are very similar. At the end of this chapter, therefore, these teachings will be compared.

What they believe

The Bible

Like their founder, Christadelphians recognize the supreme authority of the Bible. As well as attending a weekly Bible class, members follow a carefully planned course of daily Bible readings. Like evangelical Christians, they claim to base their belief and their practice on the teachings of the Scriptures. Nevertheless, they have rejected some of the most basic Christian doctrines, doctrines which Christians believe are derived directly from the Bible.

God

The Christian view of God as Trinity is outlined in the Appendix. We have tried to show from the Scriptures that the only view of God that does justice to all the facts stated in the Bible is that which, whilst acknowledging that there is one God, nevertheless recognizes that the Godhead consists of Father, Son and Holy Spirit who are, in the words of the Athanasian Creed, 'coequal and coeternal'.

This view is rejected by Christadelphians. Thomas's view (given in some detail in *Elpis Israel* and in an even more speculative book, *Phanerosis,* which has proved something of an embarrassment to some modern intelligent Christadelphians) may be summarized as follows. There is only one being, the Eternal God, whose deity is underived and who is originally immortal in every sense. Below him, however, are a whole host of Elohim or gods who were created by him before the world was made and who were put to the test by him in another sphere. As a result of this successful period of probation, during which they existed as mortal men, these Elohim have now been raised to the status of immortal and incorruptible beings. They are, in effect, secondary gods. Similarly, it is possible for today's humans to become tomorrow's Elohim. Jesus has already led the way, for though once a man he has now been raised to the nature of the Elohim.

Roberts's teaching about God was much more cautious than Thomas's and, although he did follow some of his leader's ideas, his main concern was not to speculate about the Elohim but to attack the Christian view of the Trinity. He said, 'Trinitarianism propounds – not a mystery, but a contradiction – a stultification – an impossibility.'[3] How, he asked, could God be called Father unless he preceded and brought into existence the Son? Developing another of Thomas's themes, Roberts tried to discredit the Christian view that God is spirit, that he is without body or parts. His own view was that God has a physical body with all the organs, 'that the Father is a tangible person'.[4]

Although present-day Christadelphians are as opposed to the doctrine of the Trinity as Thomas and Roberts were, they appear to be divided in their attitude to the earlier Christadelphian views about secondary gods. A previous editor of *The Christadelphian* told me, 'Generally Dr Thomas's teaching on the Elohim in *Elpis Israel* is accepted,' though he qualified this by adding that an accurate summary of the Christadelphian view is that 'there is one Eternal God, the supreme, and there are beings of angelic rank who possess immortality, but as to how and when they attained that immortality the Scriptures are silent'.[5] On the other hand, another Christadelphian writer is prepared to deny categorically Thomas's speculations and to affirm, 'He is not the supreme God among many Gods but the only God.'[6] The same writer told me, 'So far as I am able to follow Dr Thomas's arguments, I cannot say that I find them altogether convincing...and I am not alone in this.'[7]

Readers may be interested to see the similarities at certain points between the Christadelphian view of God outlined above and the Mormon view of God examined in chapter 3.

Jesus Christ

The Bible teaches that the Father sent his Son, who from all eternity has shared with him the glory of the Godhead, to be the Saviour of the world. This is part of what is involved in believing in the Trinity. Rejecting the Trinity, Christadelphians therefore take issue with Christians on three points concerning the Person of Christ, his deity, his eternity and his incarnation.

Because they believe that the Father alone is God in the full sense, Christadelphians are compelled to reject Christ's deity. This means that, although they are prepared to speak of him as divine, they regard his divinity as of a derived and secondary kind. To them, therefore, Christ occupies a position similar to that of the other Elohim, for, in Thomas's terms, he is just one of the numerous Elohim created by the supreme God who, by their previous human lives of faith and obedience, have earned the right to be raised to the divine status. This is far removed from the Bible's teaching about the Person of Christ in such verses as John 1:1 and Hebrews 1:1–9.

Christadelphians maintain, 'The Son only came into existence when the virgin Mary gave birth to Jesus.'[8] In other words, they reject not only Christ's eternity, but also his pre-existence. We saw in the chapter about Jehovah's Witnesses that members of that movement, following the ancient Arian heresy, claim that the Son of God was not eternal but came into existence at a distinct point in time. Nevertheless Jehovah's Witnesses do recognize the Son's pre-existence. Christadelphians go further than Arians and Jehovah's Witnesses, maintaining that before the first Christmas day the Son had no existence at all, except as a thought in the mind of God.

Readers familiar with the Bible will recall the great pre-existence passages of John's Gospel. The author, claiming to be a faithful witness to Christ, records him saying, 'I am that living bread which has come down from heaven' (6:51, NEB), 'God is the source of my being, and from him I come. I have not come of my own accord; he sent me' (8:42), 'Before Abraham was born, I am' (8:58), 'I came from the Father and have come into the world. Now I am leaving the world again and going to the Father' (16:28), and 'Father, glorify me in thine own presence with the glory which I had with thee before the world began' (17:5). Some modern theologians get round the implication of such verses by stating that the author is simply putting into the mouth of Jesus what the first-century church had come to believe about him. Christadelphians, though they claim to accept the Scriptures at their face value, take an even less convincing way out. These verses, we are asked to believe, indicate no more than the fact that the Son existed as a purpose in the divine will. Taking them as they stand, however, these verses indicate at the very least that Jesus was conscious of his personal pre-existence with the Father.

It is a short but inevitable step from the denial of Christ's deity and eternity to the rejection of his incarnation. If he is not God in the full personal sense, and if he did not exist before he was born of the virgin Mary, then obviously it is nonsense to speak of his *becoming* man in the sense understood by Christians. God did not become man. Moreover, Jesus did not become the Christ until he was baptized. Thereafter, all through his earthly life, say Christadelphians, he remained man. It was not until he was raised from the dead that his humanity was transformed into divinity. Contrary to what orthodox Christians believe, therefore, Christadelphians will not agree that Jesus Christ ascended into heaven as the God-man, though they do say 'he is now the corporealisation of life-spirit as it exists in the Deity', whatever that means!

Readers familiar with the history of Christian doctrine will not need to be reminded that these views of Christ's Person were current in the second, third and fourth centuries AD. Christadelphianism is a modern form of adoptionism.[9] Now, as then, adoptionism has to be rejected by the Christian church as a travesty of New Testament teaching.

The Holy Spirit

As we saw in chapter 2, Christians believe that the Holy Spirit is not a mere influence or invisible force, but a divine Person, the third Person of the Trinity. Christians believe that such a view of the Spirit's Person is necessary to do justice to the New Testament's teaching, especially in John 14 to 16.

Christadelphians deny the personality of the Spirit but admit his eternity. This is quite logical in their doctrinal system, for to them the Spirit is 'an unseen power emanating from the Deity, filling all space, and by which He is every-where present... It is the medium by which He upholds the whole creation'.[10] Christadelphians affirm that it was this power that enabled the apostles to perform miracles but claim that it does not dwell in believers today or they would be able to perform similar miracles. So Roberts states, 'There is no manifestation of the Spirit in these days. The power of continuing the manifestation doubtless died with the apostles.'[11] As we shall see, this has repercussions for the movement's doctrine of salvation, for unlike Christians Christadelphians do not believe that people are converted to Christ as they respond to the Holy Spirit at work within them.

Salvation

'Nothing will save a man in the end but an exact knowledge of the will of God as contained in the Scriptures, and faithful carrying out of the same,' wrote Roberts.[12] Against this, we are justified in asking, 'Who then can be saved?' The greatest biblical scholar would not claim 'an exact knowledge of the will of God as contained in the Scriptures'. The godliest saint would not dare to affirm that he has faithfully carried out 'the same'. Even allowing for a certain amount of hyperbole in Roberts's statement, it does indicate the direction his thoughts were taking. Salvation, he felt, resulted from the combination of an intellectual grasp of the Bible's teaching and a life of good works.

To this day, Christadelphians remain strongly opposed to the doctrine of justification by faith alone, considering it to be one of Christianity's corruptions. For them real faith is not faith in a person, the Christ of whom the biblical Thomas could say, 'My Lord and my God!', but mental assent to Christadelphian doctrines, the reception of Christadelphian baptism by immersion that goes with it, and a good life. That this is no exaggeration of their position will be seen from their view that infants and imbeciles cannot be saved, for both are incapable of indulging in this kind of intellectual exercise.

All of this is closely tied up with the Christadelphian belief that man has no inherent immortality. When animal man dies, Christadelphians believe, everything that there is of him perishes. His only hope for the future lies in resurrection. Therefore, those incapable of response (like infants and the insane) or found unworthy (through wickedness or a deliberate refusal to respond to God's Word) will not be raised.

It is not surprising to find, in view of all this, that Christadelphianism provides its adherents with no assurance of salvation. After all, if salvation depends upon what I do, rather than on what Christ has done, who may tell whether I have done enough to earn God's approval? Even baptism, though regarded as indispensable to salvation, can do nothing more than make the Christadelphian 'a lawful candidate for that "birth of the spirit" from the grave, which will finally constitute him a "son of God, being of the children of the resurrection"...His ultimate acceptance will depend upon the character he develops in this new relation'.[13]

How, then, are we to interpret what Christ did on the cross? The Christadelphian view is that the cross was simply a declaration of God's righteousness. Roberts sets the view out clearly in his book *The Blood of Christ* and uses Romans 3:21–25 to try to prove it. No student of the New Testament will wish to argue that this is not *one* aspect of the meaning of the cross, but for Roberts and modern Christadelphians it would appear to be its only meaning. Certainly, they will have nothing to do with any idea that Christ died instead of us or that he paid the price of our sin, although both are clearly taught in Scripture (Romans 5:6–8; 1 Corinthians 15:3; Galatians 2:20; 3:13, *etc*). In their view, God forgives us simply on the basis of his forbearance, if we acknowledge his righteousness and turn to him in repentance and obedience.

The kingdom

Teaching about the cross is far less prominent in Christadelphian literature than is teaching about the kingdom. When Christadelphians speak about the kingdom, however, they have in mind their own particular interpretation of prophecy. Briefly, their view is as follows. The promise made to Abraham concerning the land of Canaan will be fulfilled literally at some future date. Then the Jews will be gathered in Palestine, the ancient kingdom of Israel will be restored, and Jesus will return to reign on earth. A new Temple will be erected and sacrifices will again be offered. All the faithful will be raised and given immortality, but the wicked will be annihilated.

This emphasis of the kingdom on earth arises out of the Christadelphian view of heaven. Heaven is regarded as the abode of God, but human beings do not go there at death or at any subsequent time. When Paul says that death is departure to be with the Lord (Philippians 1:23), he is thought to refer to the time when the Lord returns to earth at the resurrection. Yet in 1 Thessalonians 4:14 Paul says 'by the word of the Lord' that when Jesus returns 'God will bring *with him* those who have fallen asleep'. The straightforward interpretation of this is in the light of Christ's assurance that he was returning to his Father's house to prepare a place for his people (John 14:2). Naturally, also, the Christadelphian view of departure to be with Christ is governed by their belief in soul sleep, which is equivalent to non-existence between death and resurrection (see chapter 1).

Christadelphians and Jehovah's Witnesses

Because of certain close doctrinal affinities between the two movements, Christadelphians and Jehovah's Witnesses are sometimes confused. It may be helpful, therefore, to notice some of the main doctrinal similarities and differences.

The two movements agree that only one Being and one Person may be called God in the full sense, and that all other divinity is derived divinity. It follows that both are unequivocal in their denial of the doctrine of the Trinity, regarding it at best as a misinterpretation of Scripture and at worst as a modern version of Greek mythology or a complete fabrication inspired by Satan. There is no place in either movement, therefore, for the orthodox Christian view that Christ is both God and man, and that he is the eternal Son of God. Similarly, the Christian view that the Holy Spirit is the third Person of the Trinity is rejected by both.

There are, however, some differences in their beliefs about Christ. Both agree that he has not existed from all eternity with the Father, but that he came into existence at a distinct point in time through a creative act of God. But whereas Jehovah's Witnesses think of the Son as God's first creative act and believe in Christ's pre-existence, Christadelphians deny his pre-existence as well as his eternity, and say that he did not exist in any personal sense before he was born of Mary.

Both movements follow the traditional view that Christ's atonement was made necessary by Adam's fall in the garden of Eden, but they limit what was lost by Adam's transgression to ordinary physical life. They agree, therefore, in rejecting belief in the immortality of the soul as an unscriptural doctrine, pagan in origin. They agree, also, that the wicked will be annihilated. For both movements, eternal life will mean a kind of physical life immortalized as a result of Christ's resurrection.

There are marked differences between the two movements' views of the nature of the atonement. Whereas the whole Jehovah's Witness concept revolves around the word 'ransom', with the view that Christ as a perfect human being became the ransom to divine justice, Christadelphians practically ignore the word 'ransom' and see the key-thought of the atonement as a declaration of God's righteousness.

Both reject the biblical concept of justification by faith and replace it with a system of salvation by human achievement.

Despite doctrinal similarities, however, the two movements are very different in other respects. In particular, whereas the Witnesses employ hard-sell tactics in their proselytizing activities, the Christadelphians work more quietly (and perhaps more effectively) through Bible exhibitions, public lectures and personal contacts. The author's experience is that, by and large, Christadelphians are more ready to talk quietly and reasonably about their faith and to listen to points of view with which they disagree.

Summary of the main doctrinal differences

CHRISTADELPHIANS	CHRISTIANS
Authority	
The Bible is the Word of God and its teaching is authoritative for belief and practice. Christadelphian publications, however, set out the line of biblical interpretation that is acceptable to the leadership and in practice this is the yardstick by which Christadelphianism is measured.	The Bible is the yardstick by which all claims to truth are to be measured. All human authorities are to be judged by their faithfulness to Scripture, which is God's Word.
God	
Christadelphians reject the orthodox Christian view of the Trinity, though they use the traditional language of Father, Son and Holy Spirit.	God is Father, Son and Holy Spirit, three coequal and coeternal Persons within the unity of the Godhead.
Christ	
Before his birth at Bethlehem, the Son of God did not exist, except as a thought in his Father's	Jesus, the eternal Son of God, took upon himself our humanity (without setting aside his deity) when he

75

mind. Throughout his earthly life, Jesus was no more than human. He was raised to divinity at his resurrection. This involves a rejection of the Son's eternity, deity and incarnation.

became incarnate of the virgin Mary. In him there are two perfect natures, the divine and the human.

Salvation

In practice, salvation appears to come through an intellectual grasp of the Bible's teaching and obedience to it.

Salvation is God's gift, not a reward for works. It comes through a personal faith in Christ, not through an intellectual grasp of Christian teaching.

Notes

[1] Bryan Wilson, *Sects and Society* (Heinemann, 1961). Though written more than twenty years ago, this book is probably still the most up-to-date current examination of the movement.

[2] In Britain the principal schismatic wings have effected a reunion (Bryan Wilson, *Religious Sects* (World University Library, 1970), p. 109).

[3] R. Roberts, *Christendom Astray* (The Dawn Book Supply, 1958), p. 77.

[4] *Ibid.*, p. 79.

[5] John Carter, in a letter to Maurice Burrell, 21 November 1961.

[6] E. J. Newman, *The God Whom We Worship*.

[7] Letter to Maurice Burrell, 20 March 1962.

[8] J. J. Andrew, *The Real Christ* (The Dawn Book Supply, 1948), p. 71.

[9] Bishop Wand described (in *The Four Great Heresies* (Mowbrays, 1967), pp. 23ff.) how the author of the Fourth Gospel found himself fighting on two fronts. On the one hand were those people who were not convinced that Jesus was divine in the full sense, and on the other hand were those who were not convinced that he was really human. Whereas the first group tended to think of Jesus as a mere man, the others thought of him as a divine apparition. Wand goes on to show how the two extremes persisted throughout the early history of the church, resulting in the adoptionist heresies on the one hand and pneumatic heresies on the other. Christadelphians are a modern version of adoptionism, for they hold that Jesus is not God in the full sense but has been raised by God to some kind of divine status.

[10] J. J. Andrew, *op. cit.*, pp. 65f.

[11] R. Roberts, *op. cit.*, p. 86.

[12] *Ibid.*, pp. 57ff.

[13] *Ibid.*, pp. 236f.

5 Health and healing

Before turning to Christian Science with its particular emphasis on health, it may be helpful to consider more generally the nature of health and healing. Christians believe that God can, and sometimes does, heal by seemingly miraculous means and they can provide an impressive array of evidence to support this view. But what shall we say when an unbeliever is healed in an apparently supernormal way? Some would argue that evil spirits bring about cures to deceive people and to lead them away from God. If we take a fuller look at health and healing, however, we may well conclude that some healings may be regarded as 'neutral', in the sense that we need not attribute them directly to God or to Satan.

The grounds on which Christians would argue such a case may be summarized as follows. God has made us in such a way that the desire and momentum of the body are towards health and well-being, so when there is failure (illness), great or small, a good doctor or surgeon tries to co-operate with the body's own wish for recovery. Why, then, should there be failure of God's ideal in the first place? The Bible answers that mankind has frustrated God's declared intention. Genesis 2 and 3 show men and women pulling away from the life they enjoyed from God and trying to take control of their lives for themselves. By doing this they introduced evil consequences into their personalities, including failures in bodily and mental health. As members of the human race, we all inherit some of these bad consequences in our bodies.

The Christian would also wish to argue strongly that as

human beings we are not just bodies. Our total personality includes mind as well as body and the two cannot be separated. This means that attitudes of mind can affect the body. For example, spitefulness, hatred, deception or guilt can be the cause of such things as arthritis, ulcers and digestive troubles. On the other hand, a mind that has submitted to God, has been cleansed by Jesus Christ, and is empowered by the Holy Spirit, can have a wholesome and strengthening effect on the whole system.

Some people would retort that this is simply suggestion and there is little doubt that suggestion can be a powerful factor in health and healing, as well as in sickness. On the one hand, the hypochondriac continually suggests to himself that he suffers from various illnesses. On the other hand, doctors use suggestion, sometimes merely through their presence but at other times through prescribing *placebos* (from the Latin meaning 'I will appease you'): the patient expects a medicine that will do him good through its chemical action, but is given some entirely neutral substance which often proves equally effective. It seems that the expectation of a cure brings about the cure by suggestion. So we refer to psychosomatic illnesses (from the Greek words for 'mind' and 'body'). The physical symptoms are there and the patient suffers accordingly but, as is often said unkindly, 'It's all in the mind.'

There was a craze some years ago for the improvement of health by auto-suggestion. The prime mover was a Frenchman, Emil Coué, who encouraged people to repeat at bedtime, as monotonously as possible, 'Day by day, in every way, I am getting better and better.' Some people found this effective.

Suggestion in its most extreme form, however, is seen in hypnotism, a practice which has been used for many purposes, including some forms of healing. No-one knows why it works as it does, but the patient becomes almost totally suggestible to the hypnotist, who can then implant suggestions of healing. In stage hypnotism, which is a serious misuse of the practice, the victim may be induced to perform physical feats that he would otherwise find impossible.

Some men and women seem to be natural healers, generally

by the laying on of their hands, a healing force appearing to pass from healer to patient. Since this ability is not confined to Christians, we may class it as natural, though rare. Some of Christ's healing miracles appear to fall into this category. We are told, for example, that when the woman who needed healing touched the hem of his garment he perceived that 'power had gone forth from him' (Mark 5:30). It is said that people with a natural gift of healing cannot heal themselves.

While healers normally work through touch, some are able to heal at a distance. This ability may perhaps be linked to the projection of mind force, by which a few people have shown that they can affect or move objects at a distance. Many experiments have been tried in recent times to demonstrate this. The subject is too complicated for us to consider fully here, though we refer to it again briefly in chapter 7 (The Psychic and the Occult).

It should be noted that any such natural powers of healing differ from the special gifts from the Holy Spirit referred to in the New Testament, especially in 1 Corinthians 12 and 14. There it is made clear that a Christian healer becomes the vehicle through whom the power of the Holy Spirit flows. Thus Paul speaks of 'gifts of healing by the one Spirit' (1 Corinthians 12:9). Similarly, we find that after the coming of the Spirit at Pentecost the disciples were able to heal in the name of Jesus Christ (e.g. Acts 4:10). Strangely enough, after Pentecost the New Testament does not record any healing that comes directly from God without a Christian intermediary, although Paul may have been looking for this when he asked for his 'thorn in the flesh' to be taken away (2 Corinthians 12:7f.). On the other hand, it is clear that, since New Testament times, Christian people have been healed in answer to prayer without a Christian healer being present. What is also clear from the New Testament is that Christians are not healed through any angel or through any believer who has passed on, a point to which we again refer in chapter 8 (Spiritualism).

Although the Bible does not categorically state this, it is a fair assumption that evil spirits can work miracles of healing. It is likely, for example, that some of the wonders performed by the two magicians Simon (Acts 8:9ff.) and Elymas (Acts

13:6ff.) were healings, since healings are always impressive. Moreover, the 'pretended signs and wonders' worked by Satan through the antichrist (2 Thessalonians 2:9) probably include healings, the word 'pretended' possibly implying that the healings are superficial and not permanent. Jesus also spoke of false miracles (Matthew 24:24), and again we assume that these included healings.

So there are differing sources of healing, ranging from the purely physical to the spiritual. We cannot say, therefore, that any group or individual who is practising healing is automatically proved to be of God and so to be accepted as 'true'. If we find supernormal healings in movements like Christian Science or Spiritualism, therefore, such healings do not in themselves prove that the movement is God-given.

6 Christian Scientists

If the average person is asked what he knows about Christian Science, he will probably reply, 'They're the people who believe in spiritual healing.' A Christian Scientist might well object to this statement, pointing out that the founder of the movement, Mrs Mary Baker Eddy, called her most important book *Science and Health*, not *Science and Healing*. 'Health' is a fuller term than 'healing', and indeed a Christian Science practitioner would distinguish himself or herself from the healers described in the previous chapter. A healer believes that there is a real illness to be healed, but a Christian Scientist believes that the concept of illness is illusory, as we shall see.

Christian Scientists have a positive and non-materialistic approach to life and have well-ordered standards to live by. Most of them belong to the educated middle and upper-middle classes and, speaking generally, the movement does not attract the poorer and less educated members of the community. Their daily newspaper, *The Christian Science Monitor*, has a world-wide reputation for reliability.

Christian Scientists are included in this book of deviant faiths because their beliefs run counter to the orthodox Christian tradition and because, like the others included, they claim to have rediscovered the original meaning of the Bible. Though claiming to accept the Bible as the Word of God, they maintain that the only true interpretation of the Bible is that given by Mary Baker Eddy in *Science and Health*. It is no accident that the book has the significant sub-title, *Key to the Scriptures*. When we turn to this interpretation of the

81

biblical revelation, we soon discover that it clashes with the faith that Christians have held down the ages.

The founder

Before discussing differences between orthodox Christianity and Christian Science, it will be helpful to know something about the Founder (or, as members prefer to describe her, the Discoverer) of the movement, Mrs Mary Baker Eddy (1821–1910). Baker was the family name, and her parents were strict New England Calvinists. In her teens Mary began to pull away from her Puritan background, embarking on a search for other religious patterns. In 1843 she married her first husband, George Glover, but was widowed within a year. Although her son, George, was born shortly afterwards, certain domestic difficulties resulted in his being unofficially adopted by a friend's family when he was seven. Because this family lived some distance from the Glover home, mother and son gradually drifted apart.

In 1853 she married a dentist named Daniel Patterson, but this second marriage proved a failure. Patterson turned out to be an unstable character and Mary obtained a divorce for desertion in 1873. Meanwhile in 1870 she began giving courses of lectures in healing. In 1877 she married Asa Gilbert Eddy, who had been one of her students and who had become a Christian Science practitioner. When he died in 1882, Mary Baker Eddy (as she was now called) announced that he had been 'mentally assassinated' by one of her rebellious students. The fear of malicious mental attacks on herself remained with her for most of her life.

Twenty years earlier, while her ideas were forming, she had come under the influence of a healer named Phineas Quimby. He had begun his work as a mesmerist or hypnotist, but had come to realize the power of mind over matter even when patients were not hypnotized. We cannot here discuss the influence of Quimby on Mrs Eddy, or, as Christian Scientists claim, the influence of Mrs Eddy on Quimby, but practitioners of mind-cure are bound to have certain assumptions in common.

Quimby had just died when in 1866 Mary had a serious

fall on an icy pavement. The medical evidence of her case is disputed, but she herself claimed that the basic principles of healing were revealed to her at this time and that she was instantly cured. From this time onwards she developed the ideas which were eventually incorporated in her textbook, *Science and Health with Key to the Scriptures.*

The first draft of this book appeared in 1875 and, after various revisions and additions, it was standardized in 1907. Now all editions have identical paging. All page-references in this chapter are to *Science and Health* unless some other title is given. Before her death Mrs Eddy was able to secure by law that at any Christian Science church service only the Bible and *Science and Health* might be read, without any preaching or exposition. This ensures absolute uniformity among Christian Science churches, eliminating the possibility of private interpretations or deviations by ministers. Authorized teachers are, however, allowed to give public lectures on Christian Science principles, and such lectures remain the most significant method of Christian Science outreach today.

Every Christian Science church contains two lecterns, one holding the Bible and the other *Science and Health with Key to the Scriptures.* As much as the legal ruling referred to above, this design feature makes clear that Christian Science (like Mormonism) looks to another written source in addition to the Bible. Although Christian Scientists deny that they regard Mrs Eddy's book as scripture, in practice *Science and Health* is treated as scripture, for the Bible is read in the light of this book.

Mrs Eddy maintained, 'As adherents of Truth, we take the inspired Word of the Bible as our sufficient guide to eternal life' (p. 497), but she also claimed in her book *Miscellany,* 'It was not myself, but the divine power of Truth and Love, infinitely above me, which dictated *Science and Health with Key to the Scriptures*... I should blush to write of the book as I have, were it of human origin, and were I, apart from God, its author. But, as I was only a scribe echoing the harmonies of heaven in divine metaphysics, I cannot be super-modest in my estimate of the Christian Science textbook' (*Miscellany,* pp. 114f.).

In spite of these high claims, the book is not easy to follow.

Although its various subjects are divided into chapters, these are muddled and repetitive. Mrs Eddy's philosophy is hard to grasp and single sentences may be misleading if they are quoted in isolation. Nevertheless, it is not difficult to find her main points of departure from orthodox Christianity.

Healings

Before discussing the philosophy of the book, we may look at the claims for healing, since (as we have said) these are what the average person regards as Christian Science. Although the book contains testimonies of healing in chapter 18, we cannot check them against medical records. Other cases are quoted in *The Continuing Spirit* by Norman Beasley. Many of the cures could be classified as psychosomatic, as indeed many orthodox Christian healings can be. Few are impressive, but Charles Braden in *Christian Science Today* refers to Mrs David Oliver of Chicago who was 'the first instance recorded of recovery from generalized blastomycosis' (p. 252). This is a fungus affection of the respiratory tract, which nowadays is treated with one of the sulfa drugs. Mrs Oliver is said to have turned to Christian Science after being given up by the doctors. On the other hand, Braden records that on occasions Christian Science practitioners have been prosecuted after their patients have died through alleged lack of proper medical aid.

Naturally one looks for a proper medical report before and after the healing, such as the Roman Catholic investigators have before them in pronouncing on cures at Lourdes. But Mrs Eddy turns the desire for evidence by saying that 'a physical diagnosis of disease – since mortal mind must be the cause of disease – tends to induce disease' (p. 370). For this reason the movement is against Christian Scientists becoming nurses in general hospitals, and dislikes health instruction for children in schools. In earlier days healing testimonies in the journals were said to have been authenticated. Nowadays they are said to have been carefully verified 'to the best of our ability'. This verification means that the healing is attested by two church members, but not necessarily by doctors.

Although Christian Scientists normally avoid doctors, on

the ground that their attitude to disease as real induces wrong thinking about it, they often appear to the outsider to be hopelessly inconsistent. Mrs Eddy herself wore glasses and dentures, and received morphine injections to relieve pain from a stone in the kidney. She allows for this as follows: 'If from an injury or from any cause, a Christian Scientist were seized with pain so violent that he could not treat himself mentally – and the Scientists had failed to relieve him – the sufferer could call a surgeon, who would give him a hypodermic injection; then, when the belief of pain was lulled, he could handle his own case mentally. Thus it is that we "prove all things; (and) hold fast that which is good"' (p. 464). 'Until the advancing age admits the efficacy and supremacy of Mind, it is better for Christian Scientists to leave surgery and the adjustment of broken bones and dislocations to the fingers of a surgeon, while the mental healer confines himself chiefly to mental reconstruction and to the prevention of inflammation' (p. 401).

If, like some Christian writers, Mrs Eddy had been content to speak of the power of positive thinking as part of the divine plan for the health of body and mind, she would have contributed something of value to the Christian church. But she dissociates her methods from all other forms of spiritual healing.

Christian Science as a philosophy

This brings us to the strange philosophical system to which the healings are linked. Basically the whole system rests on the assertion that spirit and matter are wholly incompatible. 'Spirit never created matter' (p. 335). 'Matter has no life to lose, and Spirit never dies…This shows that matter did not originate in God, Spirit, and is not eternal' (p. 275). A Christian would comment that there is no necessary inconsistency in holding that matter originated in God even though it is not eternal; indeed both the beginning of Genesis and the first verses of John's Gospel explicitly state this (cf. Mark 13:31).

Mrs Eddy, however, writes: 'Spirit is the only substance and consciousness recognized by divine Science. The material senses oppose this, but there are no material senses, for matter has no mind' (p. 278). If we ask what then matter is, her answer is, 'Matter is a human concept' (p. 469). More about the Christian approach to these issues will be found at the end of this chapter. Note, incidentally, how Mormonism comes down on the opposite side, and holds that matter is so much a reality that even God must have a material body.

It is obvious that Mrs Eddy has parted company with the Bible, since the opening chapters of Genesis clearly show that God created this very material world. Moreover the incarnation was Christ's taking of a fully material body and becoming subject to the laws of matter, by suffering hunger, thirst, pain and death. The answer of *Science and Health* is to spiritualize all references to material creation. In other words, Mrs Eddy first forms her theory, and then bends the Bible to fit it. Thus in interpreting Genesis 1:6 she says, 'Spiritual understanding, by which human conception, material sense, is separated from Truth, is the firmament' (p. 505) and on Genesis 1:16, 'The sun is a metaphorical representation of Soul outside the body, giving existence and intelligence to the universe' (p. 510). The very earthy Genesis 2 is brushed aside as 'false history in contradistinction to the true....In this erroneous theory, matter takes the place of Spirit. Matter is represented as the life-giving principle of the earth' (p. 522). We also find an extraordinary interpretation of Adam: 'Divide the name Adam into two syllables, and it reads, *a dam*, or obstruction. This suggests the thought of something fluid, of mortal mind in solution' (p. 338).

Science and Health objects to the title Jehovah, which appears in Genesis 2, asking, 'Did the divine and infinite Principle become a finite deity, that He should now be called Jehovah?' (p. 524). On the same page the worship of Jehovah is compared to the worship of pagan deities. Yet Jesus Christ himself quoted the Old Testament command that we should love Jehovah our God with all our being (Mark 12:29f.).

Mortal Mind
Matter is said to be 'a human concept' (p. 469), the product of Mortal Mind which is under the delusion that disease, which appears as an affliction of the body, is real. The term

Mortal Mind occurs frequently, but it is extremely difficult to discover exactly what it means. 'It is meant to designate that which has no real existence', we are told (p. 114). Matter is said to be 'another name for mortal mind' (p. 591). Elsewhere it is defined as follows: 'MORTAL MIND. Nothing claiming to be something, for Mind is immortal...the opposite of Spirit, and therefore the opposite of God, or good; the belief that life has a beginning and therefore an end...the subjective states of error; material senses; that which neither exists in Science nor can be recognized by the spiritual sense; sin; sickness; death' (pp. 591f.). Once again one notes that everything turns on Mrs Eddy's own idea that Spirit cannot create genuinely existing matter.

Sin and disease
Christian Science denies the reality of sin and sickness, and it is significant that these two are regularly linked by Mrs Eddy. Thus she writes, 'The only reality of sin, sickness, or death is the awful fact that unrealities seem real to human, erring belief, until God strips off their disguises' (p. 472); and again, 'Jesus bore our infirmities; he knew the error of mortal belief, and "with his stripes (the rejection of error) we are healed"' (p. 20). The phrase 'he knew the error of mortal belief' is ambiguous in this quotation, but it becomes clear a little later: 'At the time when Jesus felt our infirmities, he had not conquered all the beliefs of the flesh or his sense of material life' (p. 53). This denial of the reality of sin is made plain in another place where Mrs Eddy wrote, 'Christ came to destroy the belief of sin' (p. 473). Strangely enough, this sentence has been changed since the 1905 edition of *Science and Health* which followed the Bible with 'Christ came to save sinners'.

This astonishing interpretation of the redemptive work of Christ must be seen alongside the idea that man is not a fallen being. Thus we are told, 'Whatever indicates the fall of man or the opposite of God or God's absence, is the Adam-man, for it is not begotten of the Father' (p. 282). Moreover, 'Sin exists here or hereafter only as long as the illusion of mind in matter remains. It is a sense of sin, and not a sinful soul, which is lost' (p. 311). In contradiction of this idea the

Bible contains Christ's awful warning to 'fear him who can destroy both soul and body in hell' (Matthew 10:28). The Bible also makes clear that sin is not an illusion, but a hideous stain from which all need to be made clean (1 John 1:7).

Christian Science leaders today are naturally concerned to explain Mary Baker Eddy's teachings in a way that makes more sense. Thus a representative of the Committee on Publication wrote in a personal letter to the author, 'The words "unreal" and "real" have a distinct meaning in Christian Science. The word "real" relates only to what is *divinely* true. When, therefore, the Christian Science textbook refers to sickness as "unreal", it certainly does not imply that it has no existence in human affairs. As much space is taken up to show how cancer, tuberculosis, brain disease, insanity, *etc.* are to be treated in Christian Science, it is obvious that they are not being regarded as non-existent or unreal in a *human* sense. The thing which no doubt encouraged Mary Baker Eddy to class disease as "unreal" in the divine sense was the fact that it disappeared immediately it was confronted by the divine understanding of our Lord. So the word "unreal" in Christian Science has the definite Pauline sense that "the things which are seen are temporal" (2 Corinthians 4:18).' Similarly the writer points out that Christian Science makes people aware of their sins, which must be seen and cast out. But 'from a *divine* standpoint sin is as "unreal" to God as "three threes are ten" is unreal to mathematical principle...The word "unreal" is applied to sin as to sickness to indicate "no part of spiritual reality" rather than "no existence as a factor in human affairs".'

We have quoted extensively from this letter so as to try to understand a possible difference between existence and reality. All that can be said in response is that we do not find this difference in the Bible. Paul's words quoted from 2 Corinthians 4:18 do not deny the reality of the temporal, but rather affirm it. His point is that the temporal is impermanent (not that it is unreal) and that one day it will give place to the eternal in which already we may have a part. Neither sin nor disease is ever cured in the Bible by denying its reality: both are realities in the mind of God and man and both have to be overcome.

There is at least one practical refutation of these ideas about Mortal Mind and illness. If someone eats or drinks something poisonous, believing in his mortal mind that it is innocuous, the poison may still kill him. Mrs Eddy's ingenious explanation reads as follows: 'In such cases a few persons believe the potion swallowed by the patient to be harmless, but the vast majority of mankind, though they know nothing of this particular case and this special person, believe the arsenic, the strychnine, or whatever the drug used, to be poisonous, for it is set down as a poison by mortal mind. Consequently, the result is controlled by the majority of opinions, not by the infinitesimal minority of opinions in the sick-chamber' (pp. 177f.). One wonders how far a Christian Scientist would stretch this to cover the case some years ago when several babies died through an unknown fault in the dried milk they were given. It also seems to have escaped Mrs Eddy's thought that the argument she puts forward would also rule out the possibility of Christian Science 'cures' on the grounds that almost everyone apart from Christian Scientists believe in the reality of the sickness.

It is very difficult to discover what Mrs Eddy believed about death. She and other good Christian Scientists have certainly died, even though they believed that 'matter and death are mortal illusions' (p. 289). She appears to argue that Jesus himself did not die. His disciples believed that his body was dead but in fact 'He met and mastered on the basis of Christian Science, the power of Mind over matter', all the claims of medicine, surgery and hygiene. Because he refused to recognize death, his body remained alive until he emerged from the tomb (pp. 44f.). So far as the rest of us are concerned, our bodies seem to die and 'the corpse, deserted by thought, is cold and decays, but it never suffers... Mortals waken from the dream of death with bodies unseen by those who think that they bury the body' (p. 429). This approximates in experience to what any Christian believes without tangling it up with Christian Science philosophy.

God
God is defined as 'Principle; Mind; Soul; Spirit; Life; Truth;

89

Love; all substance; intelligence' (p. 587). 'God, Spirit, is All-in-all, and there is no other might nor mind' (p. 275).

This comes very close to Pantheism and to the Hindu concept of all separate existences as illusion. Pantheism is the concept that God is all and all is God. Mrs Eddy limits Pantheism to the belief 'that there is mind in matter' (p. 279) and 'that God, or Life, is in or of matter' (p. 27). Even though one dismisses matter as an illusion, one may still be pantheistic, if one holds that all existence is spirit, and that there is only one spirit, namely God.

Belief in the Trinity is summarized as follows: 'God the Father-Mother; Christ the spiritual idea of sonship; divine science or the Holy Comforter' (p. 331). One need not dispute the mother aspects of God's being, since women as well as men were created in the image of God (Genesis 1:27), although the Bible nowhere addresses God as Mother. The interpretation of the Holy Spirit as divine Science (*i.e.* Christian Science) has scant regard for what the New Testament teaches of his personal being.

Jesus Christ

The Christian Science concept of Jesus Christ needs some disentangling, and one must continually watch the use of the two names, Jesus and Christ. Christian Science joins the ranks of those who do not believe in the incarnation as it is summed up in Scripture. Rather, there is first a human Jesus; then at some point something is added to him, known as the Christ, or Christ spirit. A heading on page 473 is 'Jesus not God', and on the same page we read, 'Jesus is the name of the man who, more than all other men, has presented Christ, the true idea of God.' While on earth 'the eternal Christ, his spiritual selfhood, never suffered' (p. 38). There is a fuller treatment of these and similar concepts elsewhere in chapter 9 (Theosophical Systems).

One can see now more clearly the reason for the inadequate treatment of the *atonement*, already referred to. We have also seen that the resurrection of Jesus Christ is not regarded as the rising again of his material, though transformed, body from its real death on the cross. But at the ascension 'the human, material concept, or Jesus, disappeared, while the spiritual self, or Christ, continues to exist in the eternal order of divine Science' (p. 334). By contrast, the New Testament looks forward to the time when 'at the name of *Jesus* every knee shall bow...and every tongue confess that *Jesus Christ* is Lord...' (Philippians 2:10–11).

To sum up: Christian Science is scientific in the sense that it uses well-established laws for healthy and health-giving thinking, and observes sound social and individual morality. As a religio-philosophical system it takes its place among alternative philosophies, and can fairly be compared with them. But as an exposition of biblical truth it leaves much to be desired.

A Christian approach to points at issue

Spirit and matter

The Bible certainly teaches that God is Spirit (John 4:24), but it also shows that he is the Creator of this very real space-time universe, involving that which is material (Genesis 1 and 2; Acts 17:24, *etc.*). Since it requires a reversal of human experience to treat the material as unreal, it is hard to see why God should have put us all under this delusion. The Bible, in fact, regards spirit and matter as equally real. Sin and the world-system have to be overcome, not by denying their reality, but by struggling against them (*e.g.* John 16:33). It is a strange assumption by Christian Science that Spirit could not create matter (p. 335).

The nature of God and the incarnation

The Bible teaching concerning the Trinity (outlined in the Appendix) is completely different from the Christian Science view, summarized earlier. It is especially important to remember that the essential of New Testament Christian faith is not an impersonal Christ Spirit, but of the personal Son who deliberately determined to come into the world as man. So we see that on earth Jesus Christ remembered the glory that he had had previously with the Father (John 17:5). Moreover, though he was truly God, he emptied himself of his glory to become man and die (Philippians 2:5–11). Such

91

emptying was a personal act: though he was rich, yet for our sakes he became poor (2 Corinthians 8:9).

So far from teaching that 'the spiritual idea, Christ, dwells forever in the bosom of the Father' (p. 334), there was no 'Christ' before the eternal Son of God came into the world to take up the position of the Christ, for 'Christ' is the Greek equivalent of the Hebrew 'Messiah' which means 'Anointed'. 'Christ' is, therefore, the recognized title of the earthly descendant of David's line, who would one day come as Saviour. Thus Jesus himself asked the Pharisees, 'What do you think of the Christ? Whose son is he?' and they replied, 'The son of David' (Matthew 22:42). Mrs Eddy's idea of an eternal Christ spirit has no place in the New Testament, although of course all orthodox Christians continue to affirm the *Son's* eternity.

Healing

This has been dealt with in the previous chapter.

For further reading

For a good understanding of Christian Science, there is no substitute for Mary Baker Eddy's own writings, published by the Christian Science Publishing Society. As well as *Science and Health with Key to the Scriptures,* these include *Miscellaneous Writings* (covering the period from 1883 to 1896) and *The First Church of Christ, Scientist, and Miscellany* (published in 1913 by her trustees after her death). These last two books contain much informative material, philosophical, historical and anecdotal, and the last named also contains some original poems.

It is probably impossible to find a 'neutral' biography of Mrs Eddy. Laudatory books include: Norman Beasley, *The Cross and the Crown* (Hawthorn Books, 1952); *Mary Baker Eddy* (1964); *The Continuing Spirit – since 1910* (Allen and Unwin, 1957); Robert Peel, *Mary Baker Eddy: the Years of Discovery to 1870* (Holt, Rinehart and Winston, 1966); and two sequels, *Mary Baker Eddy: the Years of Trial* and *Mary Baker Eddy: the Years of Authority* (all three of which have been published as a single volume since 1977); Sibyl Wilbur, *The Life of Mary*

Baker Eddy (Concord, 1909); and C. S. Braden, *Christian Science Today* (Allen and Unwin, 1959).

On the other side, highly critical books include: Georgine Milmine, *Life of Mary Baker Eddy* (Doubleday, 1909); Edward F. Dakin, *Mrs Eddy* (Scribner's, 1930); W. R. Martin and N. H. Klann, *The Christian Science Myth* (Zondervan, 1955). An interesting work in this category is Mark Twain, *Christian Science and the Book of Mrs Eddy*, a typical Mark Twain extravaganza, printed among his collected articles and followed by a book in 1907. Stephen Leacock's Life of Mark Twain speaks of his 'queer obsession with Christian Science', which he thought 'was about to envelop the world'.

7 The psychic and the occult

This chapter is intended as an introduction to the two that follow. In a way it says too much and yet too little. The fact is that Christians should be aware of the inner reaches of the mind without necessarily having to explore them. Anyone who reads this book has a right to some intelligible information about this whole area.

In recent years, the whole world of what once was regarded as the field of cranks has been opened up by serious investigation. It has become clear that our daily lives are more than physical experiences contributed by the nerves and the brain, and that there are deeper reaches of the mind with their own ways of functioning which do not make rational sense. These experiences may come unsought, and people may not like to talk about them for fear of being thought strange.

a. Second sight

We need not look at professional 'seaside' clairvoyants to be aware that occasionally a person may have an awareness of something going on beyond the reach of sight or hearing. It may be some emotional experience or the distress of a friend. It may be the awareness of the death of someone when we have not known of his previous illness or that he has been the victim of an accident. Such an experience may come no more than once in a lifetime.

But some people, even from an early age, have this extended awareness almost as a regular experience. For example, a teenage girl, pushed into a swimming-pool, suddenly was able to see what was happening at home; and afterwards she kept this faculty of seeing at a distance for several years.

If this kind of experience happens spontaneously, it can be taken as a rare but 'natural' experience, something that is neutral in itself, that is, neither of God nor of the devil in a direct sense. Yet, like all natural faculties, it is meant to be put into the hands of God for him to use or to take away as he sees fit.

To attempt to cultivate the gift, and especially to try to make money out of it, is dangerous for some and a temptation to pride for others. As we shall see, developed second sight may be an explanation of mediumship: the medium sees and hears what is stored in the enquirer's mind and gives it back, generally in good faith, as a message from someone who has passed on.

b. Sensitivity

Many more people are sensitive to an atmosphere of houses, places and people. They seem to know, the moment they enter a house, whether it has been a happy place. One highly sensitive lady, for example, had to retreat hurriedly from an empty house in which a husband and wife had recently had a violent quarrel.

An extension of this simple sensitivity may take the form of a vision. This may account for many cases of haunting: sensitive observers 'see' some scene replayed. A Christian doctor relates how such a sensitive person, visiting a country house, saw two men fighting with swords in the hall. The owner of the house said that these were a father and son who had lived there more than a century earlier, and he said that others had also seen them. When something like this happens it is not necessary to argue that the spirits of the departed keep returning to fight their battles over and over again. Rather, it seems that their imprint on the scene is picked up by someone in a sensitive state many years afterwards. Once again, this may be treated as a neutral experience, neither good nor bad in itself.

c. Prophetic dreams

We probably all dream so many dreams that one or two are almost bound to come true. On the other hand, some people have found that the contents of a vivid dream have actually happened shortly afterwards. There are, for example, cases of a dreamer seeing the house into which the family will be moving, although at the time the place was totally unknown to him or her.

The Bible contains a few prophetic dreams: some of them are sent by God (*e.g.* Genesis 41:15; Jeremiah 31:26; Daniel 2 and 4); others are claimed by false prophets and are described as 'the deceit of their own heart' (Jeremiah 23:25–32), that is, their own unconscious. Although God may still guide through prophetic dreams (Joel 2:28; Acts 16:9), occasional dreaming of something that happens shortly afterwards is likely to be a neutral experience.

d. Travelling in time

This is very rare. The often-quoted story of the two ladies in the Trianon (Versailles), who apparently experienced people and surroundings as they had been in the time of Mary Antoinette, has been both defended and attacked; but there are a few similar cases on record.

e. Astral projection

It is rare for this to occur naturally, but recently doctors and others have been writing about patients who have apparently died under an operation but have been resuscitated. Afterwards these patients have spoken about an 'out of the body' experience, during which they saw and heard from ceiling height all that was happening in the operating-theatre. Many of them went on to tell of passing through a tunnel and coming face to face with a bright light, and of coming to a boundary fence which they knew they must either go across and die or else return to their bodies.

This is mainly what a Christian would expect, since a person has (or is) a soul as well as a body. Although the process of death itself is likely to be more than this, this semi-death makes sense.

f. Mind over matter

Uri Geller created a sensation when he came to Britain and America and, under test conditions, was able to bend keys and other metal objects without making physical contact with them. It was then discovered that several children were able to do the same in different parts of the world, even as far away as Japan. Interestingly enough, one girl who demonstrated her ability to bend metal in this way, had practised healing from the age of three. Presumably she was one of those natural healers, described in chapter 5 (Health and healing). Some adults are able, under strict control, to move objects without contact; the writer has watched films of this.

g. Ghosts

See sections *a*. and *b*. of this chapter.

h. Poltergeists

In contrast to a haunt, where everything remains the same when the ghosts have disappeared (even though, for example, doors may have been seen to open during the event), poltergeists move or throw objects or even set them on fire. When this happens it is generally the case that there is someone in the house or family who is psychologically disturbed. A poltergeist disturbance has, in fact, been described as 'having a breakdown outside the body'. If this is all there is to the experience, it is another example of mind over matter. Many believe, however, that evil or mischievous spirits are behind the phenomena. It is possible, of course, to hold both ideas simultaneously, for a spirit may make use of the psychic force generated by the person. As we shall see in the following chapter, this is how some people explain the phenomena connected with the use of the ouija board. Fortunately, very few people ever encounter poltergeists outside sensational newspaper reports of rare, genuine occurrences.

i. Dowsing

In contrast to putting out energies, dowsing involves the picking up of signals from the ground through the movements of a hazel twig or a rod when the holder passes over underground water. Some people are able to extend the scope to other things besides water, such as metal, and a few have claimed to trace lines of force travelling underground. There need be nothing unnatural or supernatural in this capacity.

The problem becomes more acute for Christians when dowsing includes the use of large-scale maps to discover the site of hidden objects. In his book, *Between Christ and Satan*, Kurt Koch gives examples of possession or obsession by evil spirits after the repeated use of the pendulum, which, when held over a map, swings when it is moved over the significant place. Similarly, a pendulum or a more elaborate device is used to diagnose illnesses and prescribe cures, and there are some practitioners who diagnose by the response of the device to a blood sample from the patient. Various 'cures' are tried until the device responds normally.

Although positive results are claimed for such methods, more investigation is needed. A few years ago a detector described as the Black Box was the subject of a legal case in which it was ruled that its claims were false. Since a pendulum or other device cannot work by itself without manipulation by someone, it may well be that telepathy and clairvoyance are the main factors.

j. Psychometry

A few people have the ability to take hold of something belonging to someone else, even someone totally unknown to them, and perceive true things about the owner or the people who have handled it. It is as though we imprint all our possessions with something of ourselves, and the psychometrist is able to get back along the 'line' to ourselves. A few psychometrists have been able to assist the police, the best known being the Dutchman, Gerard Croiset. Although police in Britain follow up any professed psychometric visions in cases of murder or kidnapping, success is very rare indeed.

One reason why a Christian will hesitate to develop this faculty, if it does not come spontaneously, is that it involves breaking into another person's life, almost as a spy.

k. Witchcraft

The next two types of phenomena are very far from neutral, having a sort of attraction similar to that of drugs. Although they continue underground, from time to time they are exposed in the media when something unpleasant emerges. Today there is a craving for power that is either the manipulation of psychic power or of power given by evil spirits or of both together. The person involved prefers to have this power rather than to commit his or her life to God's control. Occasionally a Christian may meet one of these victims, who seeks help to break away from practices which have degraded him or her.

Witchcraft claims to be the old religion that was unfairly displaced by Christianity. Undoubtedly it has a long history, since that form of it which now calls itself Wicca worships the queen of heaven and there are clear indications in the Old Testament that she was a rival of the true God, as Jeremiah 7:18 and 44:17–19 make clear.

In witchcraft, covens of witches meet in secret, either in a private house or in a secluded spot out-of-doors, to take part in a ceremony which includes the calling down of the queen of heaven to become incarnate in the high priestess. This invocation opens the door to spirits who can manipulate the psychic energies of the coven. Psychic force is generated by the witches as they link hands and circle around naked, and this force is used to create spells. The ceremony may culminate in unrestrained sex within the coven.

Not surprisingly, therefore, the Bible is emphatic in its condemnation of witchcraft and spell-casters. One of the clearest references occurs in Deuteronomy 18:10–12: 'There shall not be found among you any one who burns his son or his daughter as an offering, any one who practises divination, a soothsayer, or an augur, or a sorcerer, or a charmer, or a medium, or a wizard, or a necromancer. For whoever does these things is an abomination to the Lord.' As well as the very clear prohibition, we find in Isaiah 47:9 that God's judgment will fall upon Babylon 'in spite of your many sorceries and the great power of your enchantments'. Similarly, we find in Jeremiah 27:9 the prophet warning the nations, 'Do not listen to your prophets, your diviners, your dreamers, your soothsayers, or your sorcerers.... For it is a lie which they are prophesying to you.' There are many other Old Testament references to sorcerers, sorceresses, or sorcery, the Hebrew words being connected with the meaning of 'cutting', perhaps cutting herbs, or charms, or spells, or carving out destinies for others. Other words translated 'charmer' or 'enchantment' have the idea of binding by spells or by charms. Some such practice is described in Ezekiel 13:17–23, where through the prophet the Lord says, 'Woe to the women who sew magic bands upon all wrists, and make veils for the heads of persons of every stature, in the hunt for souls!.. Behold, I am against your magic bands...and I will tear them from your arms; and I will let the souls that you hunt go free like birds. Your veils also I will tear off... therefore you shall no more see delusive visions nor practise divination; I will deliver my people out of your hand.'

The New Testament also speaks of sorceries, the Greek word being connected with poisonous or medicinal drugs. According to the book of Revelation, the anti-Christian Babylon practises sorceries and sorcerers are ranked with murderers in the lake of fire (Revelation 18:23; 21:8; 22:15). Paul describes sorcery as one of the works of the flesh (Galatians 5:20). It is also interesting to note that one result of the coming of the gospel to Ephesus was that many who previously had practised magical arts now burned their books of magic in public (Acts 19:18–19).

Those who today become involved in witchcraft discover that its effects upon them are very serious indeed. Once a person has contributed some of his own psychic force to a spirit, the spirit will be reluctant to give it back again, and henceforth has a right of entry. Those who have turned from witchcraft to Christ often claim that spirits have continued to harass them for some time after their conversion, but they are able to testify that Christ has enabled them to resist effectively.

l. Satanism

Satanism is the lowest and most terrible of the approaches to the spirit world, since satanists select the supreme anti-god as the object of their devotion. They believe that the God who has revealed himself in Scripture and in Jesus Christ is not almighty, and that one day he may be ousted by Satan. Hence satanists believe it is wise to be on Satan's side and to help him towards victory. They have joined Milton's Satan in *Paradise Lost* in declaring, 'Evil, be thou my good.'

In their challenge to God satanists desecrate whatever is sacred to Christianity, fouling and robbing churches, digging up graves, and conducting blasphemous versions of the Holy Communion in so-called black masses. They sacrifice small animals and drink their blood, and on occasions deaths of human beings have been found to be ritual killings. Perverted sex orgies are a regular feature of their worship. There is of course nothing new in this. Jeremiah described the sacrifice of young people to Molech in the Valley of Hinnom (which later was called Gehenna or hell). From the same prophet we learn that passing through the fire meant sacrifice (Jeremiah 32:35; *cf.* 7:31 and 19:4–6).

No texts are needed to show that Christianity and satanism are utter and complete opposites.

m. Possession

Normally temptations from Satan and other spirits, as distinct from the world and the flesh, are in the form of suggestions to the mind after the manner of telepathy. When a person has invited more direct influence through practices mentioned here, he may become haunted by evil presences, nightmares and obsessive impulses. Only in extreme cases is there possession of the New Testament type, where a new personality is imposed on the normal one from time to time. Sometimes there are resemblances to some psychological disturbances, such as schizophrenia, and indeed demon possession may attach itself to and intensify inherent mental or physical instability. A psychiatrist may be able to produce alleviation of distressing symptoms without discovering the

101

root cause. On the other hand, a Christian with the gift of the discerning of spirits may be able to perceive this (1 Corinthians 12:10).

Whether it is obsession or possession, deliverance comes through the victory of Christ alone, as can be seen from passages such as Colossians 2:15 and Acts 16:18. A Christian who is confronted with such cases, therefore, should if possible seek the help of others to join him in prayer, that together they may claim Christ's authority. If the case is one of possession, it will be necessary at some point to command the spirit to depart in the name of the Lord Jesus Christ. Sometimes the battle is a long one. This is not the place to go into more detail, but the books listed at the end of this chapter provide fuller information. Exorcism should not be treated lightly, nor should one be expecting cases of possession everywhere.

It need hardly be said that the Christians who pray must not themselves knowingly be giving Satan a hold in their lives. As for the victim, when he is in his right mind and when the spirit is not speaking through him, he must at least be willing to turn to Christ, otherwise the result may be a fresh possession worse than before (Matthew 12:43–45). Care must be taken not to regard besetting sin in itself as a sign of a demon needing to be cast out. Such sin needs the confession of personal responsibility and guilt, followed by repentance and renewed trust in Christ. To seek to resolve the problem by allegedly casting out a demon implants the unconscious satisfaction that the person himself is not wholly to blame.

Summary

Some Christians may occasionally have supernormal experiences which may be accepted as neutral. If such experiences are put into the hands of God, he will either use them or take them away. If they are cultivated, there is a danger that they will fill the life and give a sense of pride that the person who has such experiences possesses a power that his friends lack. Since pride is the devil's field, such a person may find himself under the influence of Satan or his servants.

For further reading

The subjects mentioned in this chapter have been dealt with in many recent books, some more balanced than others. One might mention among serious investigators Lyall Watson, Guy Playfair, Alister Hardy, Brian Inglis, Brian Innis and Kit Pedler (whose death sadly occurred while his pre-recorded series was running on TV).

From the specifically Christian standpoint some writers have investigated the subject more fully than others; *e.g.* Gary Wilburn, *The Fortune Sellers* (Scripture Union, 1972). J. Stafford Wright, *Understanding the Supernatural* (Scripture Union, 1971). Roger Palms, *The Occult: a Christian View* (Oliphants, 1973). Morton Kelsey, *The Christian and the Supernatural* (Search Press, 1977). E. Garth Moore, *Believe it or not* (Mowbray, 1977).

The last two allow occasional mediumship.

It is best not to know too much about witchcraft. The writings of Doreen Irvine, a former witch, are significant; *e.g. From Witchcraft to Christ* (Concordia, 1973).

There are several books on out-of-the-body experiences when apparently dead. A typical one is Maurice Rawlings, *Beyond Death's Door* (Sheldon Press, 1979).

A balanced book on exorcism and the occcult is John Richards, *But Deliver Us from Evil: Demonic Dimension in Pastoral Care* (Darton, Longman and Todd, 1974).

8 Spiritualists

Spiritualism is not spiritual in the New Testament sense (*e.g.* 1 Corinthians 2:10–16), but since this is the title that its advocates have chosen, we shall use it in this book. The derogatory term, *Spiritism,* is equally misleading, since it would imply that all the manifestations come from the spirit world, and this is not so.

What is spiritualism?

Spiritualism claims to provide communication with the spirits of the departed. Usually the communication comes through a medium. He or she often goes into a trance, and consequently remembers nothing of what happens while the spirits take over the voice. It is usual for each medium to have one or more 'control spirits', often with strange names, who interpret or introduce other spirits who wish to contact someone at the seance. At other times the medium remains conscious but becomes aware of forms and voices that seem to be those of the departed who wish to communicate. Sometimes at private seances there are physical manifestations, when objects are moved. Again at some such seances forms and faces appear to build up from a semi-physical substance known as ectoplasm, which is exuded from the body of the medium. The almost total darkness in which these seances are held has lent itself again and again to deception. Nowadays it is possible to see in the dark by means of an infra-red telescope or viewer, and to take photographs with infra-red film. For this the room is lit with lamps which emit infra-red rays only, which to normal sight leaves the surroundings in darkness. Under these conditions physical mediums are reluctant to offer themselves for test.

There is also a kind of 'do-it-yourself' mediumship using table-tipping, the ouija board, the planchette, or inverted tumbler. When hands or fingers are rested on these things and questions asked, a 'spirit' answers by causing the board to move to letters of the alphabet, or by rapping or thumping the table according to a pre-arranged code.

Interest in modern spiritualism in America and Europe dates from the middle of the last century when two sisters, Maggie and Kate Fox, appeared to be the centre of mysterious rappings. They and their elder sister, Leah, set up as mediums. Later in life Maggie and Kate confessed that they had faked the phenomena, but afterwards withdrew their confession. Their minds at this later date were affected by heavy drinking, and it is impossible now to discover the truth.

Biblical assessment

Spiritualism itself goes back to the distant past. It has always flourished among animistic peoples, but it was also well known in the Near East in Bible times. A Christian assessment starts with the knowledge that it is always forbidden in Scripture. The AV did not make this clear in its reference to 'familiar spirits', which at the time were believed to be animal-like demons who acted as the servants of witches. The RSV and NIV correctly use the term 'mediums'. Rather strangely, the NEB and the Jerusalem Bible speak of 'consulting ghosts', which once again makes the warning sound irrelevant, since no-one consults ghosts as such.

There are several passages in the Law that are most emphatic, one of the most important being Deuteronomy 18:10–11: 'There shall not be found among you any one who...practises divination, a soothsayer, or an augur, or a sorcerer, or a charmer, or a medium, or a wizard, or a necromancer.' A fuller discussion of this important passage is provided in the additional note at the end of this chapter.

Despite such a clear Old Testament ban, there are some

earnest Christians who believe there is a place for Christian mediums (or sensitives) today. They commonly quote some of the minor commands of the Law and argue that, since they have been set aside, there is no need to insist on retaining the ban on mediumship. There is, however, a clear difference between, say, food laws which were repealed by Christ (Mark 7:19; *cf.* Acts 10:15) and other laws which have to do with permanent spiritual relationships. Moreover, the argument advanced in favour of mediumship would also allow Christians to use sorcery, magic and divination, which clearly would be absurd.

We must see, however, what light the New Testament throws on a possible lifting of the Old Testament ban on mediumship. We find that the spirit in the mediumistic girl at Philippi was treated as an enemy to be cast out, even though it testified to the truth of the Gospel (Acts 16:16–18). More importantly, in 1 Corinthians 15 and 1 Thessalonians 4, where Paul consoles Christians for the loss of loved ones, he does not say, as spiritualists would, 'Next Sunday our prophet-mediums will convince you of your loved ones' survival by putting you in touch with them', but instead assures them that in Christ, who has risen from the dead, they will meet their loved ones again.

Nowhere in the New Testament do we find the ban on direct communication with the departed lifted. Like the Old Testament, the New Testament speaks of false prophets. It informs Christians that the spirits have to be tested to ascertain their attitude to Jesus Christ's incarnation and deity (1 John 4:1–3). It is to be noted that the good spirit is the Holy Spirit and the bad one is some hostile or misleading spirit. The test is not concerned with establishing whether the communicating spirit is your pious grandfather, for the New Testament knows of no such communication.

There is no reason why for some purpose God should not allow a departed person to return in a visible form. He did this with Samuel and again with Moses and Elijah on the mount of transfiguration. Jesus Christ himself accepted the fact that spirits might appear (Luke 24:37–39), but said that their form was not the same as his own, since his was in his body, risen and transformed; they were still awaiting their resurrection. In the story of Dives and Lazarus (Luke 16:19–31) it is not said that Lazarus *could not* have been sent back to warn the rich man's brothers, but that it was *not right* for him to return to those who already had the clear guidance of the Scriptures.

Spontaneous appearances, then, are one thing, but attempts to make further contact come under the Bible ban. One can see three possible reasons for the ban.

1. Contact with spirits easily becomes a substitute for vital Christian experience. Spiritualists make much of a report drawn up by Archbishop Lang's Committee in 1938. This was never published, but *Psychic News* somehow obtained a copy of the conclusions, though not of the evidence, and published it as a booklet. In fact the report satisfies neither spiritualists nor evangelical Christians. But it includes these words: 'We were impressed by the unsatisfactory answers received from practising Spiritualists to such questions as "Has your prayer life, your sense of God, been strengthened by your spiritualistic experiences?"…Spiritualism may afford men the opportunity of escaping the challenge of faith which, when truly proclaimed, makes so absolute a claim upon men's lives that they will not face it, but turn aside to an easier way.'

2. Many of the apparent messages from the departed may well be drawn from the memories of the bereaved by a medium's second sight. Most people who have seriously examined the evidence for extra-sensory perception (ESP) are convinced that it can occur. One of the best-known mediums of recent times, the late Mrs Eileen Garrett, several times expressed her belief that the many thousands of communications that came through her were drawn from the subconscious minds of her clients. This does not mean that she faked them, any more than the clairvoyant fakes the pictures that seem to appear in the crystal, but the stored memories and feelings come to her from the bereaved as pictures and voices. In her book *Many Voices*, published not long before her death, she takes a completely agnostic position with regard to survival after death. If she is right – and at least she holds this opinion after a lifetime of introspective investigation – the comfort that comes to the bereaved is a

credit to their own love and affection rather than a direct communication from the departed. It neither proves nor disproves their survival, but it is in fact deceptive.

3. Those who plunge more deeply into spiritualist investigations find that the communications gradually draw them away from the essentials of the Christian faith. In the last century the Rev. Stainton Moses wrote one or two books of spirit teachings that show how he was gradually led to deny these fundamentals. This is well recognized by all serious investigators. Thus Lord Dowding in *Many Mansions* points out that 'the doctrine of the Trinity seems to have no adherents in advanced circles of the spirit world. Jesus Christ is a Son of God just as we are sons of God.' The doctrine of remission of sins through the atoning death of Christ is, he says, vigorously denied.

The rejection of these unique revealed truths brings Christianity to the level of other world religions. Yet they formed the distinctive good news of the gospel which spread like wildfire after Pentecost. It almost looks as though some enemy is anxious to cut them out in defiance of God. In fact the New Testament shows that there are these enemies, Satan and other rebel spirits. Satan struggled to keep Jesus Christ from going to the cross, since his sacrificial death was the only means of bringing man from death to life, and from darkness to light, and thus breaking Satan's hold upon him (*e.g.* John 12:31–32). In the wilderness and through Simon Peter Satan offered Christ alternatives to Calvary (Luke 4:6–7; Matthew 16:22–23). After Christ's triumph Satan and his agents continue the battle by deception (2 Corinthians 4:4; Revelation 12:9, *etc.*) and persecution (1 Peter 5:8–10).

Their deception includes false messages from above (1 John 4:1–6; 1 Timothy 4:1). Spiritualists warn against the danger of deception by evil spirits, but claim that they test the spirits as 1 John 4:1–6 orders. We discuss the exact nature of this test in the next chapter (Theosophical Systems), but the relevant point here is that the test is not to establish whether the spirit is your good grandfather or some evil spirit impersonating him, but whether the spirit in the prophet is the Holy Spirit of God or some evil spirit trying to put over some teaching that reduces Christ to purely human level.

Allied phenomena

Recently there has been a revival of interest in the ouija board. Clearly some force moves the board to spell out answers to questions when two or three rest their fingers on it. The makers do not claim more than a force that comes from one's own subconscious mind. In practice the questions are asked of some entity outside of oneself, and the answers claim to be given by some departed spirit, who often identifies himself as someone who was known to a member of the group in his lifetime. Those who move in student and teenage circles have met enough damage to personality via the ouija board or inverted tumbler to make them extremely suspicious of the real source of the messages. Some young people have been encouraged to attempt suicide. Others have had most frightening inner experiences and compulsions. At times a haunting sense of evil has hung about the environment and individual participants after seances have been held. Where Christians have been aware of this sort of seance and have prayed definitely against it in the name of Jesus Christ, the movements of the board have ceased or gone berserk. Since the board does not move by itself, the spirit must enter in order to draw on one's inner forces, and once the door has been deliberately opened, it cannot easily be closed again. In fact only the claiming of the victory of Jesus Christ can give full deliverance, but full recovery may be slow.

Life after death

It is said that spiritualism is an ally of Christianity, since it has proved survival after death. Mere survival is not what interests the Christian. Survival is not the same as the eternal life of the New Testament. It is no more than a rewriting of the well-known saying from Isaiah 22:13, 'Let us eat and drink, for tomorrow we do *not* die.' The good news of Jesus Christ was not that everyone survived death, but that the new quality life of God, eternal life, was to be found in him here and now. That is why the Christian rests on the historical fact of Christ's resurrection as his guarantee, and not upon communications from the departed. It is true that the New

Testament reveals almost nothing about the present life of the departed until they receive their new bodies at the second coming of Christ, but it does reveal that they are 'with Christ' in a state which is 'far better' than the highest bliss of earthly existence (Philippians 1:23).

Additional note on the ban in Deuteronomy 18:10–11[1]

As we have seen, this passage clearly forbids spiritualistic practices, stating, 'There shall not be found among you any one who...practises divination, a soothsayer, or an augur, or a sorcerer, or a charmer, or a *medium*, or a *wizard*, or a *necromancer*' (RSV). If the translations 'medium' and 'necromancer' are correct, and refer to contacting the departed, then 'wizard' is out of place between them. Hence the New English Bible translates, 'Let no one be found among you who...traffics with ghosts and spirits, and no necromancer'; but the weakness of this translation is that people do not traffic with ghosts. Similarly, the Jerusalem Bible has 'who...consults ghosts or spirits, or calls up the dead'.

The first of the practitioners ('medium' in RSV) is one who consults an *obh*, the meaning of which will be considered later. The second ('wizard' in RSV) is *yiddeoni*, from the Hebrew root *yadah* meaning 'to know' and hence 'a knowing one'. Is this a man, or, as the lexicon says, a familiar spirit who is believed to have superior knowledge? The idea still lingers that the departed speak *ex cathedra*, as it were. The third practitioner ('necromancer' in RSV) is literally 'one who inquires of the dead'. This should not be translated as 'necromancer', for that is a word which commonly suggests the use of a corpse for magical purposes. The word for 'dead' here is the equivalent of our 'departed', whereas two other different Hebrew words are used for dead bodies.

Yiddeoni is coupled with *obh* again in Leviticus 19:31: 'Do not turn to the *obhoth* and the *yiddeoni*', and in Leviticus 20:27 the death penalty is prescribed for anyone in whom, or with whom (both translations being possible), is an *obh* or a *yiddeoni*. It is reasonable to conclude, therefore, that an *obh* and a *yiddeoni* are very similar. Leviticus 20:6 suggests that both are sought after by a client via the person who possesses them. This is even clearer in Isaiah 8:19: 'When they say to you, "Consult the *obhoth* and the *yiddeonim* who chirp and mutter," should not a people consult their God? Should they consult the dead on behalf of the living?' Consulting *obhoth* and *yiddeonim* is here exactly parallel to consulting the departed. Isaiah even notes the change of voice that is characteristic of some mediumistic communications today.

There is also the famous incident of the woman of Endor, not a witch but a medium, who was expected to contact the departed. She is twice called 'a woman who is mistress of an *obh*' (1 Samuel 28:7). The word translated 'mistress' is a feminine of *baal*, lord or owner, and it would make good sense if the woman spoke of 'my control'. It is true that she is taken over by the spirit, but the spirit is dependent on her ownership if it is to manifest.

All these passages clearly refer to mediums who have contact with, or are possessed by, spirits. If we make a distinction between the two Hebrew words, we could fairly conclude in the light of modern mediumship that the *obh* is the regular control and the *yiddeonim* are other spirits who can be called up and who respond in voices that are different from that of the medium.

Note

[1] Much of this note is reproduced from a lecture by J. Stafford Wright published in *Faith and Thought* (1977), the Journal of the Victoria Institute.

For further reading

It is impossible to try to list the many thousands of books on spiritualism and, in recent times, the related subject of ESP.

Good surveys of the field are: G. N. M. Tyrrell, *The Personality of Man* (Pelican, 1945); W. H. Salter, *Zoar* (Sidgwick and Jackson, 1961), which is a careful summary of how much and how little has been proved by spiritualism; D. J. West, *Psychical Research Today* (Pelican, 1962), a down-to-earth critique; Charles McCreery, *Science, Philosophy, and ESP* (Faber, 1967); and Arthur Koestler, *The Roots of Coincidence* (Hutchinson, 1972), a discussion in the light of modern physics.

Two evangelical assessments are: J. Stafford Wright, *Mind, Man and the Spirits* (Paternoster, 1972) which was originally entitled *What is Man?*, and, by the same author, *Christianity and the Occult* (Scripture Union, 1971).

One of the most thought-provoking writers from the Christian standpoint is Professor H. H. Price, who, as philosopher, discusses the concept of survival, and also the relation between ESP and religious experience including prayer. His *Essays in the Philosophy of Religion* (Oxford University Press, 1972) is most stimulating.

One of the most devastating exposures of mediumistic trickery is *Magic and Mystery*, by Houdini and Dunninger (Weathervane Books, New York).

Some publications sponsored by the Churches' Fellowship for Psychical and Spiritual Studies advocate the use of mediums (sensitives), *e.g. Nothing to Hide* by Leonard Argyle.

9 Theosophical systems

Theosophy (God-wisdom) is a general title for a number of systems, which claim to hold traditions that have been handed down among initiates for thousands of years. Such systems have a high regard for Jesus Christ, some holding that he himself was initiated into their truths in Egypt. Jesus is alleged to have taught these truths secretly to his disciples, so that they do not have an essential place in the Gospel writings. The disciples then taught these esoteric (inward secret) truths to an inner circle and they became the tenets of Gnosticism.

The main systems

Rudolf Steiner, Anthroposophy and Spiritual Science
The movement founded by Rudolf Steiner is not a church, but it has attracted such thinkers and writers as Owen Barfield, A. C. Harwood, the naturalist E. L. Grant Watson, and, surprisingly enough, a former Canon of Worcester, Dr. A. P. Shepherd. Some readers of this book may have willingly given active help to the movement by supporting one of the excellent Steiner schools for handicapped children. Steiner had sensible plans for education. Similarly, Christians who are conservationists and who use organic methods for agriculture may discover that Steiner advocated these sixty or more years ago. He investigated plant and mineral remedies as well as encouraging the development of the inner life.

Rudolf Steiner (1861–1925) was the son of an Austrian village station-master. He received an excellent education and became known for his work on Goethe. He was continually concerned with the development of certain inner experiences that he had known since childhood, which we may describe as intuitive, clairvoyant, and transcending time. At one time he was associated with the Theosophical Society, but in his lectures he made it clear that he would lecture only from his personal esoteric experience.

Steiner found Theosophy too much based on Eastern religion, whereas he himself was more drawn to ideas that had originated in the West. His alternative title, Anthroposophy, does not convey much, since it means 'Mankind Wisdom': his later title, Spiritual Science, is more meaningful. Although, as we shall see, his view of Christ was unorthodox, he did honour Jesus Christ and his redemption as central. He preferred the term 'Golgotha' to 'Calvary', though of course both words (the former used by Matthew, Mark and John, and the latter by Luke) mean 'skull'.

He claimed to be able to read what is called the Akashic Record. The thought is that every event that has ever occurred exists in a form that may be perceived clairvoyantly. Steiner claimed to read in this Record the evolution of minerals, plants and animals until the stage was set for mankind. Spirit beings were able to be embodied, while retaining their spirit capacity. Thereafter, development of human beings came through repeated incarnations. Thus at death the personality withdrew gradually through several layers of existence, particularly those described as the astral and etheric. After a long stay in the world of pure spirit, Steiner claimed, the person was able to digest the good and bad things that made up his lives hitherto, and with these as his *karma* he descended into a new embryo for fresh experiences.

Meanwhile, Steiner believed, there were both good and bad spirits working invisibly behind the scenes in the world, especially Lucifer, enticing to self-sufficiency, and Ahriman, working for pure materialism.

When, then, did Jesus Christ come into this scheme? Steiner was one of those who separate Jesus from the Christ. He believed that Jesus had a normal human birth and growth until, at his baptism in Jordan, the eternal Christ united with him. As was pointed out in the earlier discussion of Christian Science, however, 'the eternal Christ' is a misnomer. 'Christ' is the earthly title given to the Messiah, but the proper pre-existent title is the Son or the Word of God. By misusing the title 'Christ' in this way, Steiner was returning to an idea that the early church rejected. The Bible shows that Jesus was the incarnate Son of God from the beginning (Luke 1:35). If the divine personality descended on Jesus at his baptism, there would either be an extra person incorporated in some way into an already existing person, or Jesus would be similar to (even though greater than) the prophets of old who were inspired by God in a spiritual way.

Steiner had an interesting belief in myths and fables and rituals of old as preparatory for the coming of Christ. There would seem to be no need to dispute this, for Jesus Christ fulfilled in history those things which had previously been the hopes of mythology.

He made much of Golgotha, holding that in his death and resurrection Christ Jesus defeated the evil powers and injected spirit life into the world that was sinking in materialism. To achieve this, Christ had to enter the lowest phase of death. Thereafter he has opened the gate for us to have new life in him, and in him to develop our inner perception through meditation.

Although all this approaches orthodox Christian belief, Christ is ultimately a created spirit, who was preserved in a sinless state until he became man without experiencing any reincarnation. He was not God as revealed in the New Testament.

The Theosophical Society

This was founded in New York in 1875 by Colonel H. S. Olcott (1832–1937) and Madame H. P. Blavatsky (1831–91). They claimed guidance from reincarnated teachers in the Himalayas. Mrs Annie Besant (1847–1933) succeeded them and was assisted for a time by C. W. Leadbeater, who later became bishop of the so-called Liberal-Catholic Church. Olcott, Blavatsky and Besant spent some time in India, and were influenced by Hinduism and Buddhism.

The stated aims of the Society are:

1. To form a nucleus of Universal Brotherhood of Humanity, without the distinction of race, creed, sex, caste,

or colour.

2. To encourage the study of comparative religion, philosophy and science.

3. To investigate the unexplained laws of nature and the powers latent in man.

Rosicrucianism

Between 1614 and 1616 four booklets were published describing the travels of a certain man named Christian Rosenkreuz (Rosycross) and his initiation into occult secrets. Originally he may have been intended as an allegorical rather than a historical character. A Lutheran pastor, J. V. Andreae, probably wrote at least one of the booklets. These writings created a sensation. There were those who wanted to be initiated, but there was no-one to initiate them and no central headquarters. The philosopher Descartes searched in vain for a genuine Rosicrucian.

In 1710 a Sigmund Richter founded the Order of Gold and Rosy Cross, and thereafter various movements adopted the title Rosy Cross in some form or another. From about 1750 Freemasonry adopted what has now become an optional degree, the Rose Croix of Heredom.

Then in 1865 Wentworth Little founded the Societas Rosicruciana in Anglia, with eight degrees limited to Freemasons. Soon after 1900 H. Spencer Lewis founded the Ancient Mystical Order Rosea Crucis. With its present headquarters in California, this is the group AMORC that advertises its postal courses. It has a rival in a less secretive group founded by Max Heindel in the present century.

An interesting modern movement was the Order of the Golden Dawn (1887), which developed as a blend of occult study and Christian mysticism. For a short time it attracted such well-known people as W. B. Yeats, Arthur Machen, A. E. Waite, Algernon Blackwood, Charles Williams (friend of C. S. Lewis and J. R. R. Tolkien). While earlier Rosicrucians devised rituals, including the discovery of the body of Rosenkreuz, the Golden Dawn looked for the development of a total attitude to the visible and the invisible world.

Advanced Occultism

This term is used to distinguish its followers from practising magicians. It is not a society or group as such, but is used to describe a religio-philosophic exploration of man and the universe, generally by free-lances, with a basis of theosophical ideas.

Higher Spiritualism

We use this term to distinguish it from the run-of-the-mill spiritualism of the local circles and churches where people hope to receive messages from departed loved ones. Some researchers have little time for such activities, but rather try to contact spirits who will speak of experiences, conditions and ideas that throw light on the whole course of man's journey in time. Such alleged communicators range from Malachi to F. W. H. Myers, and their messages are basically theosophical, though there are some differences between them, notably over reincarnation. They do not accept the godhead of Jesus.

Edgar Cayce (1876–1944)

Cayce was a devout American evangelical, who under trance was able to diagnose and prescribe for illnesses in a remarkable way. He made no claims to mediumship or spirit guidance. In 1923 his gift was exploited by a certain Arthur Lammers whose mind was crammed with theosophical ideas, which Cayce in trance confirmed. From this time onwards Cayce expounded similar ideas, including some that are very strange indeed. One may suggest that, just as Cayce in trance found an inner identification with the deep mind of sick patients, so now he unconsciously identified with the inner mind of Lammers. Since Cayce's death his trance dictations and deductions from them have been published in books and periodicals by the Association for Research and Enlightenment of Virginia Beach, USA.

Main ideas

The following are some of the main theosophical ideas:

Reincarnation

The systems differ over the number and frequency of re-births, and also over their purpose. The Theosophical Society follows the East in emphasizing the law in *karma*, according to which all our experiences in this life are in precise accord with the reward and punishment that we have deserved in all our previous lives.

What we make of our present life will be carried on to subsequent lives in a similar way. Other systems stress the multiplicity of experiences that we can gain on the way to maturity. When we enter a fresh life, we choose, or are allotted, a family situation in which we can best develop along hitherto unexperienced lines, or relearn lessons that we have failed to learn before.

One naturally asks about Jesus. Only Steiner believed that he had no more than one incarnation. Cayce under trance discovered some thirty incarnations for him, including one as Adam. The Theosophical Society and Occultists believe in Masters, or Adepts, including Jesus, who have completed all the incarnations that they need, but who may choose to remain on earth to be guides and helpers.

It is generally held that the incarnations began in the far distant past, and that the lost continents of Lemuria and Atlantis were important centres of civilized development. Steiner stresses this. Man's evolution has been guided by great spiritual beings, who had themselves evolved into an equivalent of cells in the Divine Being who is at work in our solar system. There is no common agreement over the number and frequency of the incarnations even among those who claim to have a direct perception of the previous lives of themselves and others.

In recent years attempts have been made by hypnotists to take people back into memories of previous lives. Some subjects in this highly suggestible state will easily romanticize. Others produce buried memories of what they have been read or been told. Thus the apparent memories of an American housewife of her life in Ireland in the last century as Bridey Murphy shook America in 1956, until it transpired that they were almost certainly romanticized derivations of stories she had heard from her Irish aunt when she was a little girl.

Ian Wilson, in his book, *Mind out of Time*, has not been content to take these memories at their face value. Although it is true that the person has no memories of having read or heard about the people and incidents that he claims to have experienced, yet under fresh hypnosis, when asked when and where he first encountered such and such a name or place, he or she has come up with a book or conversation that they met when quite young. One of the most remarkable (p. 126) was a person who under hypnosis produced a script in Oscan, a rare language spoken in Western Italy only up to the first century BC. The script was the so-called 'Curse of Vibia', of which the person knew nothing. Under further hypnosis it emerged that some years before he had been sitting in a library, and the student at the next desk had a book open at the Curse of Vibia. The page had been photographically reproduced on his unconscious mind. Since our memories evidently carry such exact reproduction, one can relate this to the judgment, when 'the books' (perhaps of our memories) are 'opened' (Revelation 20:12; *cf*. Luke 8:17–18). Ian Wilson gives a number of less spectacular examples, where forgotten memories have been traced to their source before they were turned into experiences of previous lives.

Where there is no evidence at all of buried memories there is yet another possibility, which one may draw from the theosophical systems themselves. This is that every event in history is imprinted on past time and can be picked up by certain people under certain conditions. One can see a special example of this in hauntings, where long-dead characters are seen or heard re-enacting parts that once they played. It is unlikely that the murderer and his victim are brought back in person on each occasion! Cayce claimed that in trance he was taken to a symbolic library, where all the volumes of an individual's life-records were stored. By extracting the volume, he became aware of all the lives that the person had passed through. We may, however, suggest that if in fact Cayce was able to slip into past time, and pick up the experiences of some individual, he then erroneously supposed that this was the client who was consulting him.

Although most apparent memories go back to previous

lives that were lived many years ago, there are cases in India where a child 'remembers' having recently been one of a family – perhaps father or grandfather – in some village in another part of the country. He describes and names his former relatives, and he is proved to be correct when he is taken to the village he names. Telepathy with his new parents is ruled out, since they have no knowledge of the other family. Yet there may be a freak telepathic link of the child with the other family, corresponding to a link of feeling which certain clairvoyants have when they speak of someone whom they do not know, but about whom they have been consulted. Some support for this theory may be found in one case where the person who seemed to be reincarnated did not die until some three and a half years after the child with the memories was born. Various cases have been examined by Dr Ian Stevenson of America.

Why should a Christian object to reincarnation? There is the plain text that it is appointed for men to die once only (Hebrews 9:27–28). But, more significantly, if the belief is true it must affect our whole understanding of life and salvation. Yet Jesus Christ nowhere introduced it into his teaching. Theosophists say that he did teach it secretly, and his disciples passed it on in secret. By such reasoning one can make out that Christ taught anything one chooses! The references to John the Baptist as Elijah are explained by Luke 1:17, where John is described as preparing the way 'in the spirit and power of Elijah'.

Jesus Christ

Most of these systems distinguish Jesus from the Christ, as also does Christian Science. The Christ may be the Logos, or Mind of God at work in mankind, so that they speak of the Christ in every man. Some regard the Christ as the supreme initiate of a certain period in the development of the universe. Some, including Steiner, accept a belief that was early rejected by Christian theologians, namely that the Christ descended in fullness on the man Jesus at his baptism. Thus there was no proper incarnation, but something equivalent to the filling of the prophets by the Spirit of God.

It is important to note the test in 1 John 4:2–3 for true or false revelations that profess to come from God. 'By this you know the Spirit of God: every spirit which confesses that Jesus Christ has come in the flesh is of God, and every spirit which does not confess Jesus is not of God' – *i.e.* an incarnation, and not a separation of Jesus from the Christ. There is actually an early variation in the Greek text and, although it is unlikely to be the original, it emphasizes the meaning of the true text and it was quoted by several early Christian writers, and in its Latin form appears in the Vulgate. This variation has, 'Every spirit which looses (or divides) Jesus is not of God.' We may interpret 1 John 5:6 in a similar way. 'This is he who came by water and blood, Jesus Christ (note both names), not with the water only but with the water and the blood.' At first sight one thinks of the blood of atonement, but in John 1:13 blood stands for conception and birth. Thus Jesus was not only designated as Messiah at his baptism when he was called to commence his public ministry, but was also the one Jesus Christ from conception. (See also the Appendix on the Trinity.)

Atonement
The Theosophical Society, following Hindu and Buddhist ideas, adopts a doctrine of *karma* (exact and inevitable retribution or reward) which makes forgiveness and remission of sins impossible. In every lifetime we reap the reward or pay off the debts of previous lives. Many spiritualists agree. Cayce and Steiner accepted *karma* up to a point, but believed that the death of Jesus Christ on the cross is central, and opens the way for forgiveness and redemption, so that bad *karma* may be broken.

Psychic powers
All these systems hold that man has latent powers which can be developed. The brochures of the Rosicrucian AMORC offer to teach their use. They include simple capacities such as hunches and intuitions, telepathy and clairvoyance, thought projection, the reading of the past and the future, and such things as astral projection.

The careful investigations of psychical research have shown that these capacities occasionally emerge sponta-

121

neously. The danger of trying to develop them is that at the least they become over-absorbing, since they give a sense of power, and at the worst they become involved in mediumship. They may even be used in witchcraft, where the covens, or gatherings, of witches generate psychic power in order to project it for their own purposes.

Spirit beings

These systems have an active belief in unseen elementals and grades of spirits, good and bad. Sometimes these spirits merely form a background of belief, as with the *devas*, who are regarded as spirits who look after the world of nature. The Findhorn Trust in Scotland claims to have personal fellowship with these spirits in their efforts to grow good food and flowers.

On the other hand there are magicians and witches who try to make use of these spirits. The novels of Denis Wheatley show something of how they work, although Wheatley himself has never taken part in magical ceremonies. There are groups who practise what is called Ritual Magic, such as the Golden Dawn, and other magicians who operate as individuals. Generally there is a blend of psychic force and the invocation of spirits, but always there is the aim of Godlike power.

It is likely that Colossians 2 speaks of magic of this kind. Paul takes the magician at his face value as one who is aiming at what is good. Hence the magician invokes angels (18) and undergoes the discipline that magicians inflict on themselves before approaching the unseen world (21). Paul attacks any practice that tries to make use of spirit beings, good or bad. His argument here is that Christ has delivered us from the elemental spirits of the universe (8, 20), those fallen spirits that try to sway the minds of men (2 Corinthians 4:4 of the supreme rebel, Satan; and Ephesians 6:12 of the world rulers of darkness). Further, in Colossians 2:15 Paul speaks of the disarming of the principalities and powers by Christ on the cross. Therefore he concludes that we are not to tamper with intermediate beings, whether professedly good or bad, since we are linked to Christ, the Head (9–10). If we are joined to the Head, what place is there for the in-betweens? The unadmitted answer is that submission to Christ means the desire to do his will; the manipulation of psychic and spirit forces means the power to do my own will.

For further reading

A fuller evangelical assessment of some of the occult forces mentioned here will be found in: J. Stafford Wright, *Mind, Man and the Spirits* (formerly *What is Man?*) (Paternoster, 1972), and *Understanding the Supernatural* (Scripture Union, 1971).

The Theosophical Society publishes its own booklets. A critical treatment of its early days can be found in John Symonds, *Madame Blavatsky: Medium and Magician* (Odhams, 1959).

Anthroposophy. The Anthroposophical Society publishes Steiner's works. A good over-all idea of his teachings will be found in a volume of essays, A. C. Harwood (ed.), *The Faithful Thinker* (Hodder and Stoughton, 1961).

Rosicrucians. H. Spencer Lewis, *Rosicrucian Questions and Answers* (Rosicrucian Library, California, 1932).

Advanced Occultism. Cyril Scott, *Outline of Modern Occultism* (Routledge, 1974).

Ritual Magic. Francis King, *Ritual Magic in England* (Spearman, 1970).

Higher Spiritualism. Raynor Johnson, *Nurslings of Immortality* (Hodder and Stoughton, 1953) and *The Imprisoned Splendour* (Hodder and Stoughton, 1957).

Edgar Cayce. The standard life of Cayce is by Thomas Sugrue, *There is a River* (Holt, Rinehart and Winston, 1942), now also in paperback (Dell, 1970). There are at least eight paperbacks of Cayce material, published in the USA, but often available in Britain.

Appendix:

The Christian belief in the Trinity

Since so many of these modern faiths reject the Christian doctrine of the Trinity, it is worth summarizing the reasons for this belief. It was not invented as an addition to the simple ideas of the Bible; but during the first three or four centuries AD the church was being continually bombarded by views of God that were based on one or two texts only. In the face of this, serious Christian thinkers were concerned to draw together all the relevant teachings of the Bible, and to crystallize them into formulae that would be a guide in interpreting individual texts. They did with the Bible what the scientist does when he formulates his laws from all the facts around him, and not simply from a few. Even when Protestants and Roman Catholics and Eastern Orthodox parted company, they all agreed that these creeds and summaries were true statements of what the Bible teaches. In recent years the rejection of the authority of the Bible has resulted in a desire to rewrite the doctrines.

So, although the Bible does not formulate a doctrine of the Trinity, yet, if we gather all the facts about God that appear in the Bible as revelation, we are inevitably led to the Trinitarian belief.

The deity of the Father
This needs no proof texts, since it is taken for granted in the New Testament, and no-one denies it.

The deity of the Son
Jesus Christ was aware of a unique relationship with the Father. In Matthew 11:27 he says that he and the Father know

each other in a way that no other person can experience. We note that the knowledge is reciprocal. Hence we are justified in seeing his claim to be the Son of God as an awareness of his divine nature. The Jews understood this, and accused him of blasphemy because, being a man, he made himself God (John 10:33). Again, they tried to kill him because he 'called God his own Father, making himself equal with God' (John 5:18). Jesus admits that the title *Elohim* (God or gods) is sometimes applied to God's deputy rulers, but says that the title, Son of God, is all the more applicable to him, since he had been consecrated by the Father and sent into the world (John 10:34–38).

It is important to notice how often Jesus Christ spoke of himself as having been sent into the world (*e.g.* John 5:23–24, 30; 8:18, 26; 16:5; *cf.* Romans 8:3). He had a previous life with the Father (John 16:28; 17:5), and so did not have the first beginning of existence at birth, as we have.

Other uses of the title 'Son of God' are significant. In the temptation in the wilderness he did not dispute Satan's use of his title (Matthew 4:1–11). The point of Satan's 'if' was not to throw doubt on his divinity, but to try to make him misuse his divine powers. It is the 'if' of argument, as in the text, 'If God be for us, who can be against us?' (Romans 8:31, AV). When demons were forced to admit that he was the Son of God, he did not deny it, but forbad them to make it known (Mark 3:11–12). He needed to prepare the minds of his disciples to reach the inevitable conclusion that he was more than mere man. To have gone round continually asserting his deity would have been too much for their minds to bear. What he aimed at was to draw out an ultimate response such as Peter made in Matthew 16:16, 'You are the Christ, the Son of the living God', although it was not until after his resurrection and the coming of the Spirit that the full significance of the title dawned on the disciples. We realize that there are passages in the Bible to which we can return and find a fuller significance in them after we have had a further revelation in Scripture.

It is important also to note that, while Jesus Christ is the unique Son of God (*e.g.* John 1:18, *etc.*), we may *become* sons of God through faith in him (John 1:12).

Whatever weight we may attach to the title 'Son of God',

there are some plain texts that certainly teach Christ's deity:

a. John 1:1. In spite of what Jehovah's Witnesses say, the Greek can only mean 'the Word was God', or 'what God was, the Word was'. The Greek word for God, *theos*, sometimes has the definite article before it and at other times stands by itself. Thus in the first eighteen verses of John 1, the form with the article occurs twice and without the article four times, in addition to verse 1. Jehovah's Witnesses single out this one occurrence in verse 1 as though it meant 'a god', rather than God in the full sense of the word.

b. John 8:58. 'Before Abraham was, I am.' This extraordinary use of the present tense can only be because Christ was claiming to have the name Jehovah (Exodus 3:14). The Jehovah's Witness *New World Translation* excels itself in evasion by translating, 'Before Abraham came into existence, I have been', an impossible rendering of the present tense.

c. John 20:28. Christ accepts Thomas's worship of him as 'My Lord and my God'. This cannot be simply a pious exclamation, since no Jew would thus take God's name in vain.

d. Philippians 2:6. The technical term, *form* of God, can only mean *having the nature of God*, or *all that constitutes God as God*. If we deny this meaning, we must also deny the manhood of Christ, since exactly the same Greek word is used in verse 7 of his taking the *form* of a servant.

e. Hebrews 1:8. Christ is here distinguished from angels and men by being given the title *God*.

f. Matthew 1:23; Luke 1:35. His conception through the action of the Holy Spirit demonstrated that he was Son of God and God with us.

These are a few clear texts, but Christ's deity underlies the whole New Testament. Thus his promise to be with all his people all the time could be fulfilled only if he is God (Matthew 28:20). He is identified with Jehovah (Yahweh) in John 12:40–41, which says that the vision of Jehovah that Isaiah saw in Isaiah 6 was a vision of Christ. Similarly Revelation 2:23 applies to Christ the claims of Jeremiah 17:9–10, that only Jehovah can search the heart of man.

If Christ is God, he cannot be a created being. He and the Father must be eternal, as is also the Holy Spirit. Thus the title *Son* is pictorial rather than genetic, and includes the concept of the One who is heir of all things (Colossians 1:15–20). Note that Christ remembered his pre-incarnation existence with his Father (John 17:5).

The deity of the Holy Spirit

To lie to the Holy Spirit is to lie to God (Acts 5:3–4). The linking of the Spirit with the Lord Jesus and the Father in such places as 1 Corinthians 12:4–6 and 2 Corinthians 13:14 would be near blasphemy if he were not himself God. The Holy Spirit is also personal. Thus he wills (Acts 13:2; 1 Corinthians 12:11); he understands (Romans 8:27); he may be grieved (Ephesians 4:30). Such terms would be meaningless if applied to an impersonal influence or power.

The distinction between the Three

At the baptism of Jesus Christ, he was in the Jordan, the Father's voice was heard from heaven and the Holy Spirit descended on him (Mark 1:9–11). Christ on earth prayed to the Father, and promised that the Father would send the Holy Spirit (John 14:26).

The unity of the Three

The presence of One means the presence of all. The Spirit of God in the heart means Christ in the heart (Romans 8:9–11). There is a wonderful sequence in John 14:16, 18, 23, where the coming of the Spirit is the coming of Christ himself, and is also the coming of the Father to dwell with the believer.

Conclusion

How can these facts be brought together? Not by postulating three Gods, since the Bible is emphatically monotheistic (*e.g.* James 2:19). Not as a single God playing three parts at different times. The only summary that meets all the scriptural statements is *three Persons in one God*. God is one, but this oneness is not a bare mathematical unity. It involves personal relationship. Even in ourselves we are aware of some shadow of this higher unity. We are one, and yet we are personal in our body and personal in our mind. My body is involved in all that my mind is, and my mind·is involved in all that my body is, but there are certain things that my mind does and others that my body does. It is proper to say that I, as my body, eat my meals, and I, as my mind, travel abroad with my ideas. Similarly it is proper to say that the second Person of the Trinity, and not the Father, became man, and his incarnation did not break the Trinity.

Those who dismiss the doctrine of the Trinity as ridiculous should be reminded that three-dimensional space is a natural analogy of what we say about the Trinity. Space requires length, breadth and height. All three are equal in importance, and none is greater or less than the others. So we have three dimensions forming one space. For some purposes we treat them as one; for other purposes we separate them.

Some people object to this formulation of the doctrine of God as being too academic. Against that view, two things can be said. First, the doctrine of the Trinity sets out those truths that God has revealed about himself. He revealed them in order that we might understand what God is like and what he has done for our salvation. Secondly, it is not being suggested in any way that an academic knowledge about God is any substitute for the personal knowledge of God that comes through Jesus Christ. If, however, we are concerned to know the truth which lies at the basis of our faith, this doctrine of the Trinity is inescapable. Everything is summed up in Ephesians 2:18: 'Through Jesus Christ we…have access in one Spirit to the Father.'